COLLEGE MATCH

A Blueprint for Choosing
the Best School for You

TENTH EDITION

BY

STEVEN R. ANTONOFF, PH.D.

OCTAMERON
ASSOCIATES

Address correspondence to:
Octameron Associates
PO Box 2748
Alexandria, VA 22301
703. 836. 5480 (voice)
703. 836. 5650 (fax)

octameron@aol.com (e-mail)
www.octameron.com

ISBN 1-57509-128-3
PRINTED IN THE UNITED STATES OF AMERICA

Table of Contents

Preface 5

To Parents: How to Use this Book 8

A Note to Counselors 10

Chapter 1: Your Power to Choose a College 12
    College Choice as a Process 14
    The Lucky 13 Myths About Choosing a College 15
    Beginning to Dream 19

Chapter 2: Knowing Yourself 21
    Worksheet 1—Self-Survey for the College Bound 22
    Worksheet 2—Scoring/Interpreting Your Survey 29
    Worksheet 3—Activities/Experiences Record 41
    Worksheet 4—Your Admission Profile 44

Chapter 3: What Are You Looking for In a College? 50
    Worksheet 5—Qualities That Will Make a College Right for You 51
    Worksheet 6—Characteristics of Your Ideal College 68

Chapter 4: Building Your College List 71
    Arriving at Your Initial List of Colleges 71
    Worksheet 7—Colleges You Are Considering 77
    Comparing Your College Choices 77
    Worksheet 8—College Fact Finder 80
    Guidelines for Determining Your Likelihood of Admission 89
    Worksheet 9—Your Apply List 92
    Application Completion: Keeping on Track 92
    Worksheet 10—Application Timetable 94

Chapter 5: Learning from Campus Visits 97
    Common Questions About Campus Visits 97
    Worksheet 11—Campus Visit Notes 106

Chapter 6: Making Your Essays Work for You 114
 Before You Start 114
 Worksheet 12—Tackling Sample Essay Questions 116
 Worksheet 13—Essay Brainstorming 125
 Hints for Excellent Essays 129

Chapter 7: The Admission Process Revealed 131
 Be Yourself 132
 Factors Important in Selecting Students 133
 Behind the Scenes 136
 Dealing with Admission Decisions: Accept, Reject, Wait List 137

Chapter 8: Being Successful in Your Freshman Year 140
 Attitudes 140
 Academics 142
 Using Resources 142
 Course, Majors and Careers 143
 Other People 144
 Controlling Time 144
 Other Areas 146

Chapter 9: Parents As Educators in the College Selection Process . 147
 Commonly Asked Questions 148
 Your Proper Level of Involvement 153
 Some Specific Suggestions 155
 Dealing with Rejection 157
 Final Comments 158

Appendices:
College Planning Goals
 Freshman and Sophomore Years 160
 Junior Year 162
 Senior Year 165

Possible Major Fields of Study 167

Potential College Activities List 168

References for College Planning 169

PREFACE

■■■■■■■■■■■■■■■■

College Match is intended for use as a workbook and guide in the
process of choosing a college. I have used, tested and refined the information and materials in this workbook throughout the last twenty years of work
with students. I wrote this book because I did not find another guidebook or
set of materials that systematically and comprehensively aided the process
of choice. It does not pretend to have all the answers to the issues faced by
prospective college students and their families. But it does, I believe,
provide perspective and guidance and, further, gives college shoppers a
framework upon which to base solid choices.

Four important principles guided the writing of this book.

First, all students, regardless of grades or test scores, have colleges from
which to choose. Students merely need to seize the opportunity and realize
that choices do exist. Through the use of this book, along with proper
guidance and support, all students will find colleges where they will be
successful. While it is true that admissions to college has become much
more competitive in recent years, it is also true that the collegiate opportunities in the United States are tremendous.

Second, the college choice process neither has to be, nor is inherently,
stressful. While some students and their parents are anxious about selecting
a college, much of that stress comes from false assumptions about the
nature of college admission. Once students and their families replace the
quest for "the best college" with one focusing on "the best fit," the level of
tension will be reduced significantly. While this book covers both "getting
in" and "fitting in," it focuses on "fitting in" because I feel this should be
the primary emphasis throughout the college selection process.

Third, there is a sequence of steps that, if followed, will lead to solid,
suitable college choices. This book is organized around those steps.
Systematically moving from one step to the next will lead to self and college
awareness. These awarenesses are the "stuff" upon which students should
base their college choices.

Fourth, finding a college builds important, lifelong skills in initiative-
taking, decision-making and responsibility. For many students, choosing a
college is their first real-life choice. By making difficult decisions during the

college choice process, and accepting the consequences of their decisions, students will also gain a great deal of self-understanding.

To celebrate this, the tenth, edition, some notable changes have been made. A few of the items in the "Self-Survey for the College Bound" have been changed and the interpretation better reflects the college planning issues faced by students considering their college readiness. Also revised for this edition is the worksheet, "Qualities that will make a college right for you." The revision of Chapter 4 contains more specific information about the process of finding good fit colleges. Such material should give students the tools they need to identify and compare their college choices. Finally, the essay chapter has been revised to contain the most common essay topics.

Whatever changes were made here, the essence of the book, and its general parameters remain much as it has from the beginning. The book's interactive nature, particularly the inclusion of the worksheets, enables students to participate actively in choosing a college. Such involvement leads to better, more satisfying decisions. The Self-Survey, the central component of Chapter 2, is widely used and remains one of the few attempts to systematically explore the variables that ought to be considered by students as they begin their college search. In recent years, it has been used by *U.S. News and World Report* as part of their college planning website.

Overall, *College Match* offers students encouragement (laced with realism) throughout the entire college choice process. When students are empowered with the knowledge that they have real options from which to choose their futures, they will feel confident and positive.

I owe a huge debt of gratitude to Maric Friedemann, the book's original coauthor. Many of the concepts and perspectives Marie provided continue on these pages—and will for as long as the book exists. Marie's sensitivity toward students, her keen eye and ear for college planning issues, and her clean, active writing style are at the core of *College Match*. She remains a colleague and a friend. Any success of *College Match* is a tribute to her efforts. For this edition, Patricia Lackner worked with me on the revisions of the worksheets and she read drafts of the new sections of the book. She brought clarity to many issues and I thank her for her efforts. Thanks also to Anna Leider at Octameron Associates who for almost two decades has found a place for *College Match* amid many options. The book would not be in your hands without her.

College Match was inspired by the hundreds of students with whom I have worked. They have helped me in the preparation of these pages. Every worksheet has benefited from the critical eyes of my students. More importantly, each student has, in his or her own way, opened my eyes to another issue, another possibility, another frame of reference involved in college choice. I have learned from each of them and, if my perspective is on-target, it is the result of their contributions to my thinking. And because I am always learning, I want to know the extent to which this book works for current readers.

As you begin choosing colleges, I hope you do so with openness and enthusiasm. Also, I hope you will know the power of choice, and with it, you will choose schools where the best in you will be revealed. I am anxious for your feedback and encourage you to e-mail me at eduadvise@comcast.net.

Steven R. Antonoff, Ph.D.

Certified Educational Planner

eduadvise@comcast.net

Denver, Colorado

Spring, 2009

To Parents

How to Use this Book

This book is written for students because I believe students should assume responsibility for the college search. But I am sensitive to the depth of parental concern that surrounds the college selection process, and we have written this book to guide parents in their important role, too. The following tips will guide you through these pages.

Parents should read Chapters 1 and 8 first. These two chapters provide important perspectives about the college search.

You can assist your student by encouraging him or her to move, sequentially, through the chapters. The chapters are organized according to the way the college planning process most logically unfolds. Students should read one chapter at a time, completing any worksheets in that chapter. Chapters 2, 3 and 4 present the most central material and, thus, more time should be spent on them. Of course, there may be reasons to alter the order. If, for example, you are planning to visit college campuses, you should read Chapter 5 immediately. If your student is worried about college essays, he or she will find help in Chapter 6.

College Match includes thirteen worksheets, each building on the preceding one. Parents can review the worksheets after each is complete, adding insights as necessary. Each has a specific purpose. For example, Worksheet 2 enables the student to better understand himself or herself as an upcoming college student. Worksheet 5 delineates the factors your student believes to be important in choosing a college. Worksheet 5 should be shared and discussed as a family, and you should not hesitate to add factors you feel should be considered in the process of college selection. Some of the worksheets are personal and ask the student to probe his or her background and readiness for college. Such self-assessment can be difficult, and some students find sharing these kinds of personal insights with anyone, parents included, awkward. But a nonjudgmental attitude and trust will go a long way toward better communication.

The following general guidelines/suggestions may be useful:

1. Students should be encouraged to take the college planning process seriously. It is neither a game nor an exercise. It is a process of thinking, reflecting, researching and choosing. And it takes time. You can't expect to find a college in a day. It is often laborious, and patience is as necessary here as it was when your child learned to walk or ride a bike.

2. Students need to understand the ambiguity that comes with making important decisions. In the case of finding a college, there are no absolutes, few "rights" or "wrongs," and lots of conflicting information. Parents can assist their student by stressing that a solid college choice will be made if he or she methodically moves from one phase of college identification to the next.

3. Parents, like their students, should seek the help of experienced counselors. A competent and sensitive counselor will bring clarity as well as knowledge to your college shopping—and may defuse many familial conflicts, as well. Most importantly, the counselor, using the results of the worksheets in this book, is vital in identifying appropriate colleges for consideration.

4. Students are encouraged throughout the book to seek the opinions and perspectives of their parents about different topics. But you may want to give your student a gentle nudge every now and then to share viewpoints and feelings. I hope the book opens lines of communication and gives both parents and students a useful base of knowledge. During the most important college planning months, you should set aside one hour per week to talk about these issues.

5. Throughout the process, attempt to support your son's or daughter's good research skills. Good research includes asking lots of questions, reading, examining oneself and separating college facts from college lore. Help your student use the resources outlined in Chapter 4.

6. Expect a lot from your student, but be mindful of the difficulty of the teenage years. Adolescence is a time of conflicting feelings and perspectives; simultaneously, teenagers are independent and dependent, mature and child-like, all-knowing and yet knowing nothing. They are at once ready to leave for college, yet desirous of the security of home and family. Take time to discuss these issues and feelings as they arise.

You have in your hands a blueprint for finding a college. Armed with this information, you should feel empowered to guide your student through the process.

A NOTE TO COUNSELORS
■■■■■■■■■■■■■■■■■■■■■■■■■

The voice of an experienced counselor brings our words alive for the college-bound student. And you will note that I have often directed the student to seek your counsel.

Unlike the outlook presented in many books and on many websites, I think the college planning and admission processes are not characterized by easy answers, fool-proof formulae, or sure-fire strategies. This is not a book of suggestions for "packaging" an applicant whose only goal is to "get in" to a "name brand" college. Because it provides neither recipes nor guarantees, it is, I believe, more in keeping with the way the college admission process, indeed life itself, unfolds. And, hopefully, it is more in keeping with your own philosophy.

I believe this book can be used effectively in busy college counseling offices. In fact, it may serve as a student text for a course in college planning or a series of workshops for juniors and seniors. The material is equally suitable for one-on-one meetings.

While the topics proceed in sequence, the chapters need not necessarily be used in the order in which they are laid out here; indeed, each school counseling office will determine the suitability of the chapters (and the worksheets) according to the needs and goals of its own counseling program and the specific population of students it serves.

Perhaps most importantly, this book is designed to maximize your time. Students who use the worksheets and read the text will come to you having reflected on themselves as well as those factors or qualities important in their college choice. They will come to you having given thought to essays or visits or other matters. And, having used the worksheets with hundreds of my own students, I believe them to be "student friendly"—with questions, instructions and interpretations that are self-explanatory and even interesting. When students come to you with this preparation and content, your time with each student can be utilized meaningfully on the most salient college counseling issues.

I have learned much from the writings and the practices of the many school-based and independent counselors with whom I have worked. This book reflects those insights, but my desire to learn continues. I am eager to hear your opinions on the issues raised in the book and on the ways in which those issues are developed. My e-mail address is found in the Preface.

The world of higher education is a rich one indeed, and we (public or private school counselors and educational consultants alike) share in the mission of opening up each student's eyes to that world. I hope this book contributes to that mission.

CHAPTER 1

....

YOUR POWER TO CHOOSE A COLLEGE

This is a book about choice. Choice is not a simple word. Our lives are filled with an endless array of choices. We ask such questions as: What will I wear today? Should I strive for As and Bs or be comfortable with Bs and a couple of Cs? What will I have for lunch? What courses should I take in school during my senior year? How much commitment do I want to make to sports or to my school work? Will I be in a good or bad mood today? Some choices are relatively simple, others are quite complex. Some affect our lives in a major way, others have few consequences. We make hundreds of choices in the span of even a single day. And not making a choice is a choice as well! The consequences of our choices can be good or they can be bad. They can be positive or they can be negative.

Picking a college is an important choice—perhaps the most important choice you've ever made. Your choice of a college can either be good or bad, positive or negative, depending upon your willingness to devote yourself to the process. If you invest yourself in the search, you will find many schools from which to choose. If you are passive and wait for your counselor or parents or mailbox to bring word of "the perfect school," chances are you'll be sadly disappointed with your ultimate choice.

So much has been written about "getting in" to college that students often seem surprised when the word "choice" is associated with college planning. Today, almost every student, regardless of academic record or family resources, can experience the joy of choosing from a wide variety of schools. Perhaps the most difficult task is truly believing you have the power to do so. Are you ready to begin the exciting process of making college choices?

Students often feel their choice of colleges is extremely limited. If they have not received all A's, if their high school classes are not the most competitive offered, or if their scores on SATs or ACTs are below average, they may feel they do not or will not have choices—or at least that they will not get into a "good" college. How wrong these students are. First, as you will see, the definition of a "good" college is terribly subjective and imprecise. It tends to mean colleges about which you or your family have heard. But of the 4,000 or so colleges in the United States, with how many is a typical family really familiar? Very few. Second, however you choose to define "good," hundreds of "good colleges" exist. So be free to explore. Open yourself up to discovery.

There is a reverse side to the phenomenon just described. Instead of feeling they have too few choices, some students feel they have too many. Parents are often enthusiastic and thrilled by all these choices. A student, however, may be confused and even believe "it would be better if I didn't have a choice." The process can become frustrating, especially since as students, you may be just learning the skills and strategies necessary to make good decisions. Just remember, at the beginning of the college search, your task may seem overwhelming, but, with patience and perseverance, your early frustration will pass, and ultimately, result in better college choices. So don't take the easy way out and just settle for one college or another. Explore.

Your first choice is whether you desire a college education. Some students simply assume they will go to college and do not go through the important process of contemplating their lives without a college education. Many business and corporate leaders, to take one segment of society, do not have college degrees. Yet, they are happy and often financially successful. Be assertive in making your decision to go to college. Articulate why you want to go. It's not enough to say, "I need a college degree to get ahead." (Interestingly, there are some recent studies that dispute this notion.) Instead, you should have the desire to learn; there should be subjects about which you want to know more. Articulating the values of a college education will enable you to appreciate the benefits of your education. To aid your thinking, make a list of the outcomes you desire from a college education. Think about how you want to be different as a result of going to college.

Another choice involves deciding whether you want to be a student. Often, students claim they want to go to college, yet they don't show the requisite commitment to the academic side of college life. They may see college as four years of fun and games. While college is filled with a great many social opportunities, college attendance is primarily an academic decision. Are you ready to make a commitment to your studies? Do you have the persistence necessary to be a successful student? Firmly deciding to be a student is important as you contemplate college attendance.

Assuming you're committed to pursuing a college education and to being a student, your next choice is when you want that education to begin. Some students delay the start of their college experience for a year or more to be prepared fully—emotionally as well as intellectually—for the rigors of college education. The so-called "gap year" or "time out" programs are increasingly popular. Many students spend productive years traveling, working or tackling internships or service projects. And research shows that students who take a year or so between their high school experience and the start of their college career are better prepared to meet the challenges of their college years. Still other students make the choice to begin their education at a two-year college, developing basic skills and confidence, before entering a four-year college. And there are students for whom a trade, vocational or technical school fits their needs perfectly.

You may feel several emotions as you embark on the task of selecting a college. You may feel happy with your successes in high school and look forward to four wonderful years in college. You may feel regret or anger that you didn't earn higher grades in high school. You may feel terror or panic at the complexity of finding a college that meets your background and personality. You may feel overwhelmed because there are so many colleges from which to choose. Or, you may feel more than one of these sentiments.

Finding a college should not and need not be traumatic or stressful. You can look at your college choices in a positive or in a negative way. Let's take an example. Suppose Jenny is told she can probably get accepted to 3,900 of the possible 4,000 colleges in the United States. If Jenny is prone to negativism, she would say, "Heck, I might not get into 100 colleges and that bums me out." Instead, she should look at this situation in the appropriate, positive way and say, "Wow, 3,900 colleges want me and I can be successful at all of them!" Optimism and perspective are important as you begin to look for a college. Remember, 90% of the colleges in the U.S. accept over 80% of those who apply.

The diversity and excellence of United States colleges are truly mind-boggling. In fact, our colleges are widely regarded as the best developed in the world. Your investment in the college selection process is the first way to demonstrate your commitment to your future success. It's a unique opportunity to affect your life in a positive way.

College Choice as a Process

Picking a collegiate atmosphere in which to spend four years is best viewed as a process, a series of steps in which each builds on the previous one. It is necessary to take your time and carefully complete each step before moving on to the next. That is how this book is designed. You start with an analysis of yourself as a potential college student. You then review the qualities that will make a college right for you. You next use all of the resources at your disposal to select the colleges to which you will apply. Finally, after hearing from your colleges, you move to the last step: picking your college.

The essential premise of this book is that by going through the steps as outlined, you will have excellent colleges from which to choose. But you need to be an active participant in the process. You need to take your selection of a college seriously. You have to be open to new information and put aside any stereotypes or preconceived notions about colleges in general or about individual colleges. You need to be open to valid information from wherever it comes. You need to be organized. (Appendices A, B and C will help you keep track of important college planning goals.) You need to consult with people who know you and who know colleges. It's a big decision and while you should direct the total effort, you should also heed the advice of those who are assisting you.

Lucky Thirteen Myths About Choosing a College

For some reason, the college admission process seems to be a breeding ground for inaccurate perceptions and faulty statements. Students and families often hear comments that are made with the best intentions, but which often are not based in fact. Here are thirteen myths about the college selection process:

Myth #1: "Colleges are either good or bad."

Nonsense. By what criterion is a college good or bad? In whose eyes is a college good or bad? Academic quality is not easily assessed and, while some colleges are better known than others, it is not true that these colleges are good and the rest are bad. The key question is *not*, "Is X a good college?" Rather, the question is, "Is X a good college *for me*?" Look for colleges appropriate to your educational background, your goals, your ability and your personality. Equally inaccurate is the notion that, "If I don't recognize the college name, it's probably not a good school." Guard against relying on stereotypes in looking for a college. The "best" colleges are not by definition in the East, for example. And contrary to a popular stereotype, there is great fun to be had at small colleges. Also be careful of relying on word of mouth: "Aunt Betsy went to Stony Bay College and loved it so I would like it too." No. Colleges change and you are not the same person as Aunt Betsy. Erase preconceived notions about colleges. Start with a clean slate.

Myth #2: "Future employers and graduate schools give an edge to those who have degrees from prestigious universities."

Not necessarily. As the general level of quality in colleges has risen over the last several decades, and as more and more colleges have distinguished themselves, employers and graduate school admission staffs can no longer rely on the name of a college as the most important selection factor. What *is* important is your success in college. As a result, wise students are matching themselves to colleges within which they have the potential to make good grades and contribute positively to campus life. Such students, with distinguished records in college, are highly sought by company recruiters, graduate schools and professional schools. Five years out of college, a person's own qualities will decide whether she gets a raise. Do Ivy League graduates have a lock on lists of the most successful individuals in our society? The richest? The happiest? The most humanitarian? There is no evidence to suggest any of these questions are true.

Myth #3: "Colleges always choose the 'best' students."

Nope, it's not true. College admission staffs work long and hard to choose students, but no foolproof or magic formula exists. Furthermore, what does 'best' mean? Their decisions are human and, hence, open to interpretation and judgment. Colleges consider so many variables as they decide on admissions: courses taken, scores, grades, extracurricular activities, as well as geography, athletics, kids of faculty members and a host of other variables. Admission directors often say that in any given year, if they had to go back and make their decisions all over again with the same candidate pool, they would often choose different students to receive letters of admission. So students should be certain their final college list is well balanced in terms of admission difficulty. (In other words, students should apply to some colleges where their admission chances are so-so, and some colleges where their chances are quite good.)

Myth #4: "Schools that cost more are of higher quality."

Why would this be true? A college education is expensive even at a state university. That one college costs double or triple what another school costs says a lot about the size of its state subsidies and its endowment, very little about quality of the undergraduate program, and nothing about whether the college fits you! Many factors go into determining the fee structure of colleges. Students should look at how well a school matches their own college selection criteria (see Chapter 3) and make few judgments about quality on the basis of cost. If you find a college that offers the right environment for you and costs a bit less, hooray! You are a good researcher of colleges.

Myth #5: "The more rigorous the admission standards, the higher the quality of education."

This relationship is tenuous at best. There are many reasons a college might have high admission standards. State universities commonly feel an obligation to in-state students and thus out-of-state admission may be quite restricted. A college may have been mentioned in a national magazine, or its football team may have gone to a Bowl game, so applications—and admission requirements—have increased as a result. Some colleges describe their mission and their requirements so well that few apply who are not appropriate for the college; hence, while they may accept a high percentage of students, they maintain a very high level of admission competitiveness. More to the point, however, is the fact that quality of education is often not directly related to admission standards. Many superior colleges do not have particularly difficult admission requirements.

Myth #6: "Cost is really important in determining where I can go to college, so I will likely have to attend a local school."

Again, not necessarily. Billions of dollars are given to students and families annually to help defray—or in some cases completely pay for —a college education. The federal government, states, individual colleges and thousands of public and private organizations make funds available to college students. Again, research is the important strategy. Investigate colleges carefully and use the resources mentioned at the end of the book to help you and your family search for either lower priced colleges or those where you're likely to receive money to help lower the cost of your education. Don't give up before you've even begun!

Myth #7: "Test scores are the most important criterion in college admission."

Not true. Colleges, now more than ever, are using a wide variety of criteria in choosing students and these are discussed in Chapter 7. The quality of the courses you've taken in high school and your grades in those courses are valued most highly by colleges. In addition, your extracurricular activities and college essays are important. Interviews, while not as significant as they once were in the selection process, are still utilized at some colleges, particularly to alert colleges to your level of interest. Also important are any special qualities you might bring to a college campus. While it is true that some large state university systems rely on an "index" that may use test scores as a central variable, most college decisions are made using many different factors.

Myth #8: "There is only one perfect college for me."

Perfect colleges rarely exist. All colleges have good and bad points and all vary in terms of the attractiveness for any individual student. Your goal is not necessarily to find the perfect college; rather, your goal is to research and find several colleges that best meet your needs.

Myth #9: "I'm a failure if I don't get into College X."

It's hard to convince students that this is not an appropriate way to think about the admission process. There are many reasons why students are not accepted at a particular college. Your academic record may not be as strong as that of other applicants. Or College X may be looking for a particular set of traits and you do not have—through no fault of your own—those particular traits. The college may, for example, be seeking tuba players or a student from a rural background and you may play the violin and be from the city. The reasons for your denial from College X are unimportant. What matters is that you are at a college where you can use your talents, be challenged in class and have a successful experience. If you plan well, you will have such choices.

Myth #10: "Some secret strategy can get me admitted to college."

No way. No strategy—secret or open—automatically unlocks the admission door. Disregard books that suggest otherwise. Students who seek letters of recommendation from a Senator or the head of a major corporation (who typically don't know the student) or join clubs in which they have no real interest are trying to strategize. Students have been known to agonize for days over an application essay without realizing it's not the topic that matters, as long as you answer the question. Students should be themselves as they seek admittance to college. Don't try to "package" yourself in wrappings that are not you. Avoid gimmicks. Trying to gain admission through strategic maneuvering or Machiavellian plotting often results in a major backfire. College admission officers quickly see through these misplaced energies. Choose colleges that fit, not colleges where you feel your fate depends on sophisticated application strategies.

Myth #11: "Relying on magazine lists of "Best Colleges" is the best way to determine whether a college is right for me."

Being so desperate for information, some students give great weight to college rankings in magazines and newspapers. But colleges are multifaceted enterprises. One size does not fit all. The qualities that make a college right for you might not be a quality that is measured by the magazine authors. In other words, no ranking considers the "feel" of a college: its atmosphere or what the students are like. No ranking considers every academic field. No ranking measures student engagement in or outside of the classroom. Far better is to rely on the people and the resources described in Chapter 4 in order to find the "best" colleges for you.

Myth #12: "If I don't know what career I'll pursue, I can't really choose a college."

The fact is, there is only one chance in 10 that a person will be doing anything connected with his/her major 10 years out of college. If you know what you are likely to major in, fine, that may help to narrow your choices. If you don't know what career is best, it's OK. Think of what else you want in a college: what type of academic experience? what type of social experience? what are the kids like at your ideal college? These and other types of questions will be discussed in Chapter 3. (Even though you don't need the answer to your career choice, high school is a good time to consider many career possibilities—to research the vast universe of vocational options.) College choice, after all, is not only about life after college. It is also about life during college. Find a place where you will be happy.

Myth #13: "A good college is hard to get into."

No. There are hundreds of "good" colleges. The more I have traveled to colleges, the more fine colleges I have found. In fact, a good match college is often easy to get into. A brand name college is often hard to get into.

Beginning to Dream

Start the college selection process with a sense of freedom. Open yourself up to the excitement and the opportunities ahead. Explore colleges in an atmosphere unblocked by preconceptions or myths.

Dream of the future—your success in college and your success in life. Discard the shackles of negativism. Don't think: "I haven't done that well in high school," "I'm not going to have many college choices," "My test scores are going to prevent my getting into college," "I'm not as good a student as my sister," "I'm never going to live up to my parents' expectations." Instead, think about the possibilities you will have by carefully examining yourself and your goals and by thoroughly exploring which college options are right for you. This attitude will lead to success not only in choosing a college, but in meeting your other lifetime aspirations.

The college experience will require you to exercise your whole being. You will be called upon to think critically and creatively, to be original, to make relationships among new ideas and concepts. Dream of what you can become academically and about the personal and professional value of your new learnings and insights. But college is more than just academics, it's the time for growth in other areas. Dream of cultivating leadership skills, enhancing communication skills, and developing a greater sense of others and yourself. Dream of acquiring practical skills like living on a budget, managing time and lessening stress. Dream about career options so you will feel better about your ultimate career choice. These dreams are the foundation of a successful college experience!

Your first step in transferring your dreams of a successful college experience into reality is picking a college that possesses the right combination of ingredients. The next chapter is designed to start you on that road. Choosing a college will take work, thought and contemplation. But it will be an important lesson in decision-making and reality testing. The right college is where your dreams can begin to unfold.

CHAPTER 2

■ ■ ■ ■ ■ ■ ■ ■ ■ ■ ■ ■ ■ ■ ■ ■ ■ ■ ■ ■

KNOWING YOURSELF

Yes, you start the process of choosing a college with a careful look at yourself, not with a list of colleges. For it is your own assessment of your interests, your attitudes, and your abilities that is central to finding a college. Why? Because the purpose of college-hunting is to find the right match between you and your eventual college choice. Many students want to start their search by looking at specific colleges. This sounds good, perhaps, but it is a faulty strategy. Before you start poring over viewbooks and catalogs from colleges, you want to examine yourself as a person and as a student. Such an appraisal will yield data about yourself that will allow you to move with confidence and greater knowledge to the next stages of finding a college.

The Four Worksheets

The four worksheets in this chapter provide an important beginning to that search. *Worksheet 1—Self-Survey for the College Bound* contains 80 items designed to assess self-awareness which, ultimately, will help you select the colleges to which you will apply. Complete Worksheet 1 when you have a few minutes; not when you are rushed. You may also complete it online at *U.S. News.* Look for "The College Personality Quiz" at usnews.com.

When you finish the Self-Survey, complete *Worksheet 2—Scoring and Interpreting Your Survey.* The scoring is easy; your interpretation will be more time consuming, but worth the effort because it will help you make connections between your responses on the Self-Survey and your potential college choices.

Next, complete *Worksheet 3—Your Activities/Experiences Record.* This worksheet allows you to list significant involvements inside and outside of school. It will help you remember your activities and accomplishments, and it will become handy when you start to prepare your college applications. Be sure to list anything and everything you have done after the eighth grade.

Finally, move to *Worksheet 4—Your Admission Profile.* This worksheet lets you see your strengths as a college applicant and enables you to judge realistically how you compare with other candidates for admission.

Worksheet 1—Self-Survey for the College Bound

Respond carefully to these questions about your educational attitudes, goals and perspectives. Be truthful and genuine and answer each question. Keep in mind, there are no "correct" responses. For each item, check the appropriate answer category—"very true," "sometimes true," "not sure" or "not true." Even if you are unsure of an answer, or your response falls somewhere between two categories, check only one answer per question.

Item	Very True	Some- times True	Not Sure	Not True
1. There are several social issues or "causes" in society about which I care deeply.			X	
2. I often participate in class discussions.	X			
3. I enjoy reading.		X		
4. I feel I know myself pretty well.	X			
5. I'm excited for my college years to begin.	X			
6. There are at least three things I can do better than others around me and at least three things others can do better.	X			
7. If I don't understand something in class, I typically feel comfortable asking my teacher a question.	X			
8. School is fun.		X		
9. I normally am enthused about the classes I am taking.		X		
10. I can identify at least one school subject or topic about which I am truly passionate.			X	

Item	Very True	Some- times True	Not Sure	Not True
11. I believe one of the most important reasons to go to college is to get a job.	X			
12. I want to organize myself so I have time for both homework and for out-of-class activities.	X			
13. I love learning for the sake of learning.		X		
14. If I want to do something on a Saturday afternoon, I usually don't need my friends to do it with me.			X	
15. I am satisfied with my listening skills in my classes.	X			
16. I can truly say I enjoy school.		X		
17. I will enjoy college a lot more if I can see how my classes apply to real life.		X		
18. I am interested in and feel comfortable talking about current events.	X			
19. Going to college means growing, learning, changing: In other words, it is not just "the thing to do."	X			
20. I enjoy learning things on my own (and not just for a class).		X		
21. I enjoy hearing and discussing other students' ideas in class.		X		

Item	Very True	Some-times True	Not Sure	Not True
22. I see college more as a time for preparing for a career than for discovering my academic interests.			✕	
23. A college with a blend of studying and socializing is important to me (even if I'd need to sacrifice my grades a little bit to enjoy college).			✕	
24. Even if my friends weren't there, I would still like school.			✕	
25. My friends and I enjoy discussing concepts and new ideas.			✕	
26. My parents don't have to remind me to study or do my homework.	✕			
27. My English teachers commend me on the quality of my papers and written assignments.	✕			
28. Making others happy is one of my primary goals.		✕		
29. Most of the time, I feel others understand me.		✕		
30. On most homework assignments, I do everything that needs to be done.	✕			
31. I am comfortable making some decisions without my parents' input.	✕			
32. I want to commit at least part of my life to bettering society.		✕		
33. Unless I have decided on a career, it will be hard to choose a college.		✕		

Item	Very True	Some- times True	Not Sure	Not True
34. On most days, I look forward to going to school.		X		
35. Assuming there was a campus speaker on an interesting topic I knew little about, I'd likely attend.			X	
36. I am the sort of person who is comfortable going outside of my comfort zone.			X	
37. There is more to college than going to class and doing homework.	X			
38. I'm usually good at prioritizing my time to get my studying done.	X			
39. I usually find class discussions stimulating and interesting.	X			
40. Learning about many different academic subjects—history, English, math and so on— is interesting to me.			X	
41. I usually initiate my own social activities.			X	
42. I tend to lose interest if class material is not relevant to the real world.				X
43. By late summer, I'm eager to go back to school.		X		
44. The college philosophy "work hard/ play hard" appeals to me.			X	
45. I see many benefits in going to college.	X			

Item	Very True	Some-times True	Not Sure	Not True
46. I seek out ways to demonstrate my concern for political/national/ international issues.			X	
47. I seldom get "tongue-tied" when trying to express myself.	X			
48. Taking lots of different subjects in college (English, math, history, etc.) is not as appealing to me as focusing on those subjects I like.			X	
49. I usually go beyond class require-ments, not because I have to, but because I am interested in the class.			X	
50. I like colleges that emphasize pre-professional programs (pre-med, pre-law, pre-business, etc.).		X		
51. I want to go to college as much as my parents want me to go.	X			
52. It is easy for me to identify my favorite class in school.				X
53. When I know the answer to a question in class, I typically raise my hand.		X		
54. I do not feel pushed into going to college.	X			
55. I am not afraid to take a position with which others will disagree.	X			
56. One of my top goals is to develop a philosophy of life.		X		

Item	Very True	Some-times True	Not Sure	Not True
57. One of the prime reasons to go to college is to meet people who will be influential in helping me get a job later in life.			X	
58. I like a challenge, but I don't want to be academically overwhelmed in college.		X		
59. I can explain why I want to go to college.	X			
60. I like teachers who encourage me to think about how academic subjects interrelate.		X		
61. I am ready to begin thinking about my future and planning for college.	X			
62. In college, it will be important that I have time to spend with my friends.	X			
63. Learning by discussion is more fun than learning by listening to a teacher lecture.		X		
64. I read about news, politics and international affairs in the newspaper or on the Internet.		X		
65. It is not that important for me to look and act like my friends.		X		
66. When I walk into class, I feel prepared and ready to share what I know.		X		
67. Thinking about one of my weaknesses is not uncomfortable for me.		X		

Item	Very True	Some-times True	Not Sure	Not True
68. The thought of going to college doesn't scare me.		X		
69. I'm pretty good at making decisions.		X		
70. Writing essays and papers is relatively easy for me.	X			
71. Building good rapport with teachers is important to me.		X		
72. I am willing to study hard in college, but I also want time to be involved in activities.	X			
73. As far as intelligence, I want the other kids at my college to be similar to me.		X		
74. I can easily identify the special qualities my friends like about me.			X	
75. If asked, I could easily list two or three words that describe me.	X			
76. My note-taking skills are good.	X			
77. I believe I know how to motivate myself to be successful in school.	X			
78. I am comfortable with my reading speed and comprehension.		X		
79. I seldom get homesick when I'm away from home for a few days.		X		
80. I enjoy volunteering my time to help people in need.		X		

Worksheet 2—Scoring/Interpreting Your Survey

Scoring your answers is easy if you follow these steps:

1. Go back to the first page of your Self-Survey.
   Above the words "Very True" write a 9.
   Above the words "Sometimes True" write a 6.
   Above the words "Not Sure" write a 3.
   Above the words "Not True" write a 0.

2. Each of the questions you answered corresponds to an overall theme relating to you as a person or to you as a potential college student. The categories are listed below. For each of your questions, enter your score in the appropriate blank space. For example, start with the category called "School Enthusiasm." Notice that the first item in that category is item number 8. By looking at your answer, you will enter one number: 9, 6, 3 or 0. Go through and fill in all of the blanks below.

3. Total your score in each category.

School Enthusiasm	Participant Learner
8. 0	2. 9
9. 0	7. 9
16. 0	21. 0
24. 3	39. 9
30. 9	53. 0
34. 0	63. 0
43. 0	66. 0
52. 0	71. 0
Total 42	Total 27

Affection for Knowledge

10. 3
13. 0
20. 0
25. 3
35. 3
40. 0
49. 3
60. 0
Total 30

Basic Academic Skills

3. 0
15. 9
27. 9
38. 9
47. 9
70. 9
76. 9
78. 0
Total 66

Independence

14. 3
26. 9
31. 9
36. 0
41. 0
55. 9
65. 0
79. 0
Total 54

Career Orientation

11. 9
17. 0
22. 3
33. 0
42. 0
48. 3
50. 0
57. 3
Total 30

Social Consciousness

1. 3
18. 9
28. 0
32. 0
46. 3
56. 0
64. 0
80. 0

Total 45

Self-Understanding

4. 9
6. 9
29. 0
67. 0
69. 0
74. 3
75. 9
77. 9

Total 57

Academic/Social Balance

12. 9
23. 3
37. 9
44. 3
58. 0
62. 9
72. 9
73. 0

Total 54

Eagerness for College

5. 9
19. 9
45. 9
51. 9
54. 9
59. 9
61. 9
68. 6

Total 69

What Do the Categories Mean?

What does each of the categories mean? What follows is a description of each of the categories. Read through them so you understand what each stands for and, therefore, consider the meaning of your scores. Remember that this survey and the interpretation that follows are intended to encourage you to think about yourself as a college student. By looking at your scores and reading the interpretations, you should be able to glean insight that will help you as you move through the college planning process.

There is no "answer" to what a specific score in a category means for you. In each category, you will see words like "scores in the mid 30's or higher suggest . . . " and "lower scores suggest . . . . " This lack of specificity is purposeful because there are many ways scores can be evaluated. It is up to you to read the descriptions and to determine what, if any, meaning a particular score has to you. Your score in one category might give you insight into something important and your score in another category might be less meaningful.

Finding meaning in high scores is a bit easier than doing so for lower scores. The first paragraph in each category provides an interpretation of the meaning of a higher score and the second paragraph is an explanation of lower scores. As stated, there is no precise meaning of a lower score. For example, for school enthusiasm, the first paragraph interprets scores "in the mid 30's or above." The next paragraph is an analysis of the meaning of "lower scores." A lower score could be, on the school enthusiasm category, anywhere from 0 to the mid 30's. Your score might be toward the lower end of the continuum or it could be toward the top. Thus, your interpretation of the category will be different if your score was a single digit or in the teens as contrasted with a score in the high 20's or low 30's. In other words, the description of a low score might be more true of you if your score was a 6 as compared to a 29.

Don't get caught up in the numerical aspects of the interpretation of your scores. The goal here is to provide information that can serve as a springboard in your quest to find colleges that are a good match for you. "High" and "low" numbers are less significant than using the information here to contemplate your unique cluster of college planning attributes.

School Enthusiasm

Those who score in the mid 30's or above often feel comfortable with the tasks and central qualities of school. In general, they like going to classes and have positive feelings about the academic nature of school.

If your score is lower here, there are several possibilities. You may enjoy some of the social features of school more than the actual classes, teachers, and classroom information. You many not have found school to be a successful academic experience, and your struggle with school may affect your attitude toward it. Your school attitude may impact your feelings about planning for college, your willingness to enter a challenging college environment, the level of competitiveness you prefer, as well as your motivation to stay in school. Do you have the motivation to be successful in college? You may not have enjoyed high school because particular characteristics of your school may not have been right for you. If that is the case, you have a chance to choose the college you will attend carefully. Your analysis of factors important in selecting a college (Chapter 3) will be particularly important in finding a college you can be excited about attending. Finally, consider these questions: Is the time right to enter college? Would you benefit from a year of travel, work or some other activity before entering college?

Participant Learner

If your score in this category is in the mid 30's or higher, you likely want to take an active, rather than a passive, approach to learning. You are not comfortable merely taking notes and regurgitating the teacher's lectures. You want to get involved. You normally do the homework your teachers assign, not only because you have to, but because it helps you learn. Likely, you participate in class discussion, enjoy it, and learn from your peers. You read the textbooks and might even read an extra book about a topic in which you are interested. Learning and understanding are so important to you that you are assertive in asking questions of teachers and fellow students. You will likely be most comfortable in colleges where professors are readily available and lecture classes are not huge. In addition, you will want opportunities for discussions and seminars as part of your college experience. High scorers should consider smaller colleges.

Lower scorers have several factors to consider. You may be interested in and committed to learning, but may prefer to learn quietly and deliberately. You may not need to participate verbally in class to learn course material. Course lectures, reading and out-of-class assignments are normally sufficient ways of learning for these students. In fact, class size will not be as significant a factor. Lower scores here may suggest a person who is better able to tolerate large classes. Hence, large-sized colleges may meet your needs.

Affection for Knowledge

If you scored in the 40's or above here, the life of the mind is exciting to you. You might read widely about a variety of topics and you enjoy learning for the sake of learning, not because you may get a good grade. You enjoy talking about ideas, philosophies and trading new perspectives. These students will look to academic challenges and to colleges that will stimulate their minds. You should be aware that big name colleges are not the only ones that provide intellectual stimulation. There are dozens of colleges that are intellectually stimulating (and not just those in the Ivy League Athletic Conference). For some students, looking at non-traditional colleges that do not stress grades is worthwhile.

Lower scores suggest that you are less comfortable with intellectual ideas and concepts. You may not have been exposed to compelling topics, issues or ideas. You may not have had experiences that have excited you about learning. You want to be cautious about applying to a college that expects you to have a serious academic focus immediately. You may want to use college as a place to try classes or subjects with which you are unfamiliar; you may be pleasantly surprised by how interesting a new subject can be. On the other hand, you might prefer a college where the classes are more directly applicable to your interests.

Basic Academic Skills

Student who score in the 40's or above are typically comfortable with the skills particularly valuable to success in college—writing, reading, note taking and prioritizing. Such students usually find college to be a bit less demanding because they are secure with the strength of their academic skills.

There are several considerations for the student who has a lower score in this category. You may want to work to find colleges where some extra assistance from teachers is readily available. You may want to exercise care and judgment when selecting English classes in college and you may want to seek opportunities where you can best develop your study skills. You may also want to guard against taking too many classes with heavy reading requirements during freshman year. On the other hand, lower scores may reflect a student who is overly critical of their own skills—but are fully able to handle the academic demands of typical freshmen courses.

Independence

Taking charge of one's own life is assessed here. College students choose their own class schedules, their own social "do's and don'ts" and their own hours. Students who score in the 40's or above will likely be comfortable with such freedom. They are less apt to act in irresponsible ways while away from home and, further, are less in need of their friends' approval before making important decisions. They will have little difficulty at colleges where there is a great deal of freedom in choosing classes and in setting your own dormitory rules. Because of your self-sufficiency, you may not need the "excitement" of a college in a large city since you will be able to generate activities for yourself even at an isolated college locale.

Those with lower scores may need more structure to be most comfortable. You may feel more at home with a series of required classes; you may prefer a college with a range of planned activities and things to do. Further, you may need to work on self-discipline or practice assuming responsibility for decisions and their consequences. A smaller college might encourage you to build your self confidence and independence. On the other hand, you may merely be transitioning from dependence to independence.

Career Orientation

Students whose scores in this category are in the 40's or higher often see college as a means to an end; in other words, these students look at college as a way to get to other lifetime goals—often, to positions of professional and vocational competence. They look at college as a vehicle for vocational preparation. As such, they will want to explore professionally-related majors and seek colleges where they will be able to keep "on track" toward meeting the needs of their chosen careers. Such students should review general educational requirements at colleges of interest. Too many required humanities courses, for example, may be less appealing than the freedom to concentrate on subjects of interest early on.

A lower score is common in this category and reflects a student who wants a general, broad based college education. You are likely very open to a wide variety of learning experiences that college may bring. You may look at college as a time for academic experimentation; where you can test a variety of ideas and career paths. You may want to explore traditional liberal art colleges with many options in the humanities, social sciences and sciences. Whether it's liberal arts or something else, you are on track to discover your likes and dislikes in college.

Social Consciousness

Scores in the high 30's and above suggest you care about the world and may not be satisfied with the "status quo." Your concern about the state of the world may influence your life and you may want to find outlets for your compassion and empathy. High scorers may want to look for colleges with political action committees, volunteer opportunities or other activities geared to reaching out beyond the bounds of campus. Some colleges place an explicit value on recognizing one's responsibility to the world.

Students whose scores are lower in this area may not be sensitive to or aware of the numerous opportunities for social responsibility. You may be comfortable pursuing your individual goals or you may have other priorities. Lower scores don't mean you don't have a social conscious! It may merely reflect that, at present, the drive for helping others is less salient than other motivators in your life.

Self Understanding

Those who score in the high 30's and above are typically in touch with their own good and bad qualities. You are fairly comfortable with who you are and don't let others direct your thoughts and behaviors. You are accepting of yourself. Your self-awareness will aid you in adjusting to college and in making decisions once you enroll. You will be less prone to behave in college as to impress others. You are comfortable with your abilities and personality and such comfort will enable you to make mature decisions in college.

If your score was lower here, you may be just beginning to know yourself. Normally, teenagers' perceptions of themselves are heavily influenced by peers. Is it possible that you are overly responsive to the wishes and demands others have for you? Your focus on pleasing others may override your personal wants and needs. You might find it easier to acquire self-understanding and confidence at a smaller, more supportive college than at an enormous university. You might look for schools where you'll be a big fish in a small pond. Lower scores are not necessarily bad! This is a skill that is a lifetime in the making.

Academic/Social Balance

Scores in the high 30's and above suggest a student who places priority on both academics and extracurricular experiences. You will want to choose a college where you will have a balanced life; that is, where you will have time for both your academic pursuits as well as extracurricular activities and personal time. You will want to look for colleges known as having a "work hard/play hard" philosophy. You should consider colleges within which you are very likely to be similar academically to the majority of other students. You should consider your college choices carefully—being certain you are not getting in "over your head." You will want to choose a college where you are as likely as anyone else to understand the material in your classes, to spend about the same amount of time studying and to be able to have a life outside of the classroom. In researching of colleges, look carefully at the characteristics of students who enroll—what were their grade point averages? Test scores? Have they taken courses in high school fairly similar to the ones you have chosen?

There are several ways to interpret a lower score here. Maybe you put a high priority on academics and want college to be all about learning. Or maybe you put a high priority on your social life and want college to be all about having fun. If you place high priority on academics alone, you may be comfortable at a college that is academically intense. If you value social experiences highly, you will want to choose colleges where you will have time to get involved in campus activities and time for your friends.

Eagerness for College

Students whose scores are in the high 30's and higher anticipate college in a favorable way and are looking forward to the collegiate experience. Adjustment will likely be easy as your enthusiasm will be a great asset in learning to master college life. While you may have some concerns about college, in general your attitude is positive. Because you played a primary role in deciding to attend college, you likely have specific goals regarding the appropriate use of your college years.

There are many reasons for a lower score and such scores don't mean you are not "college material" or that you are not looking forward to the college experience. In fact, eagerness for college ebbs and flows during the high school years. But a lower score is worth thinking about. Are you motivated to attend college? You will want to give special consideration to the ways you can make college a satisfying and productive experience. Some fears about college, leaving home and being independent are perfectly normal, so if you had a lower score in this area, involve yourself in the planning and decision-making processes and you will feel more in control and less like you are being pushed into college. But think carefully about, and seek assistance with, the timing and the nature of your college years.

What Do My Scores Tell Me About Choosing a College?

Good work. You have now scored each of the categories and learned what each means. Look back on the categories where your scores are highest and where your scores are lowest. Keep in mind that a self-survey such as this one, relying on numerical results, is inherently flawed. The self-survey is only meaningful if you use it to think about the issues presented in the categories in order to help you build your college list in a productive, informed way.

The following questions pertain to your scores. The questions will allow you to analyze, clarify and understand what your scores mean as you begin the task of choosing your college.

1. List below the three categories in which you received the highest scores:

   Highest score category _____

   Second highest score category _____

   Third highest score category _____

2. In your own words, describe what your *highest* score category says about you and your college-going needs.

   _____

   _____

   _____

   _____

   _____

   _____

   _____

3. In your own words, describe what your *second* highest score category says about you and your college-going needs.

   _____

   _____

   _____

   _____

   _____

   _____

   _____

4. List below the two categories in which you received the lowest scores:

     Lowest score category _____

     Second lowest score category_____ _____

5. In your own words, describe what your *lowest* score category says about you and your college-going needs.

     _____

     _____

     _____

     _____

     _____

     _____

     _____

6. Look at your score in the category "Basic Academic Skills." What does your score indicate about your writing, reading, note taking and prioritizing skills? How do you assess the academic skills you will need to be successful in college?

     _____

     _____

     _____

     _____

     _____

     _____

     _____

7. Look at your scores in the categories "Affection for Knowledge" and "Academic/Social Balance." How would you describe the amount of pressure that is right for you in college? Do you need/want a highly intense academic environment?

---

8. Look at your score in the category "Participant Learner." What does it indicate in terms of size of the college that is right for you? Which is better, smaller classes or larger classes?

---

9. Look at *all* of your scores. What have you learned about yourself that might be helpful in assessing your strengths and weaknesses as a potential college student? Did you learn anything else about yourself that may help you in "fitting in" to a college?

Worksheet 3—Activities/Experiences Record

I. List your in-school and out-of-school activities. Examples: student government, drama, publications, sports, clubs. List them *in order of their importance to you.* (Use additional sheets if necessary.)

Name of Activity	School Years Involved 9	10	11	12	Hrs/ week	Wks/ year	Positions Held
WORK @ DAYCARE		X	X	X	6		volunteer/employee
ASB			X		5		student
softball	X	X			12		player/captain
BABYSIT/WORK w/ KIDS	X	X	X	X	6+		babysitter
volunteer CDM		X			4+		volunteer
volunteer ACS			X		2+		volunteer
Best Buddies	X				1		

II. Creative work, hobbies, interests, or anything else not listed above to which you have devoted substantial time.

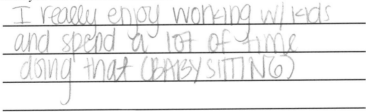

I really enjoy working w/ kids and spend a lot of time doing that (BABYSITTING)

III. Travel. Describe where you have traveled in the last three years.

All around California

_____

_____

_____

_____

_____

IV. Academic Honors. Describe any scholastic distinctions or honors you
have won, in grades 9-12. List the grade level for each. Examples: Honor
Roll—11, 12; Certificate in French—10.

9, 10, 11 grade I have been on
the honor roll.
9 & 10 grades I had 4.0 both
semesters
11 grade over 4.0 both semesters

_____

_____

V. Other honors or distinctions (athletic, literary, musical, artistic, or other).

1st place in ART show for —
my painting on a 3D design
papier mache project

_____

_____

_____

_____

VI. Employment ?

Nature of Work (clerk, delivery, etc.)	Employer (Name of company)	Dates of Employment	Approx. Weekly Hrs

VII. How have you spent the last two summers?

Last Summer

volunteered @ American cancer society shop, work at a daycare, Babysit a lot

some travel

Previous Summer

volunteer @ children's Discovery museum, volunteer @ Daycare, Babysit

some vacation

Worksheet 4—Your Admission Profile

This worksheet will help you assess your strengths as a college applicant. It provides insights for all students, but it is most valuable for students considering colleges with very selective admissions. It lists qualities admission committees feel are important as they review applications, which in turn can help you see how you might compare with other applicants. Some questions are factual and others are subjective. Your straightforward responses and your best judgment will allow you to evaluate yourself realistically as a candidate for admission.

Note: In sections I through VII, the very strongest, most attractive (to the colleges) preparation is marked with ①, the next strongest is marked with ②, the next strongest with ③. Remember, most colleges in the United States are relatively easy to get into. Even students who are ③s on this scale have plenty of colleges from which to choose.

I. Coursework. Check the number of years of coursework (grades 9-12) you will have completed upon graduation for each subject listed. In other words, project years (classes) through four years of high school by making one check per subject.

A. English

_____ 4 years (includes at least 2 in writing) ①
_____ 4 years (less than 2 years in writing) ②
_____ 3 or 3 1/2 years ②
_____ 2 or 2 1/2 years ③

B. Mathematics (Algebra, geometry, trigonometry, math analysis, pre-calculus, calculus)

_____ 4 years ①
_____ 3 or 3 1/2 years ②
_____ 2 or 2 1/2 years ②
_____ 1 or 1 1/2 years ③

C. Foreign Language (remember, for grades 9 through 12 only)

_____ 4 years ①
_____ 3 or 3 1/2 years ①
_____ 2 or 2 1/2 years ②
_____ 1 or 1 1/2 years ③
_____ 0 ③

D. Social Studies (history, government, psychology, etc.) (Geography)?

_____X_____ 4 years ①

_____ 3 or 3 1/2 years ②

_____ 2 or 2 1/2 years ②

_____ 1 or 1 1/2 years ③

E. Science

_____ 4 years (includes 3 lab courses) ①

_____ 4 years (includes 2 lab courses) ②

____X____ 3 or 3 1/2 years ②

_____ 2 or 2 1/2 years ②

_____ 1 or 1 1/2 years ③

F. Have you taken a year of art, music or theater?

____X____ Yes ①

_____ No ②

II. Class Rank. Check where you rank in relation to the other students in your graduating class. If your school does not rank students, make an educated guess.

____X____ Top 3% ①   Between

____X____ Top 10% ①

_____ Top 33% ②

_____ Top 50% ②

_____ Lower 50% ③

III. Test scores to date. Check appropriate columns for tests you have taken.

SAT Critical Reading

_____ 700 or above ①

_____ 650-690 ①

____X____ 560-640 ②

_____ 460-550 ②

_____ 450 or below ③

SAT Mathematics

_____ 700 or above ①

____X____ 650-690 ①

_____ 560-640 ②

_____ 460-550 ②

_____ 450 or below ③

SAT Writing	ACT Composite
_____ 700 or above ①	_____ 32 or above ①
_X_ 600-690 ①	_____ 29-31 ①
_____ 500-590 ②	_____ 25-28 ②
_____ 490 or below ②	_____ 22-24 ②
	_____ 21 or below ③

IV. Extracurricular Activities. Review Worksheet 3, Your Activities/Experiences Record. Check the statement that *best* describes the extent of your involvements.

_____ Extensive record of involvement in activities and/or individual talent of an extraordinary nature. Recognition extends beyond the local school or community and/or perceived as one of the most outstanding persons in the school or the community. ①

_____ Intensive leadership demonstrated in a major school or community activity (editor-in-chief of newspaper, president of student council, etc.) and/or individual talent recognized as superior. Substantial recognition for achievements. ①

_____ Significant leadership position or major participant in school or community activities and/or one or two very fine individual talents. Appropriate recognition for achievements. ②

_____ Some leadership positions or memberships in several clubs or community activities or a significant individual talent. ②

_____ Few in- or out-of-school involvements. ③

V. Basic Academic Tools. In assessing these basic tools, think about the following areas:

• Your note-taking ability.
• Your ability to read with speed and comprehension.
• Your ability to write with clarity and substance.
• Your ability to research.

You may feel better about one of these, not so good about another. But in your best judgment, and compared with other students, check the one item below that seems most true of your basic academic tools.

_____ Excellent in basic academic skills. ①
_____ Good in basic academic skills. ②
_____ Average in basic academic skills. ②
_____ Below average in basic academic skills. ③

VI. Study Skills and Time Management. In assessing these qualities, think about the following.

- Your ability to complete assignments on time.
- Your ability to set and meet deadlines for papers, for review of class material and so on.
- Your ability to handle pressure.
- Your ability to focus on what needs to be done.

While you may be better in one area and weaker in another, check the one item below that seems most true of you.

_____ Excellent in study skills and time management. ①
_____ Good in study skills and time management. ②
_____ Average in study skills and time management. ②
_____ Below average in study skills and time management. ③

VII. Academic Recommendations. Check the one set of words and phrases most likely to appear in your teacher recommendations:

_____ "best student I've ever taught," "unbelievably curious," "a real scholar," "Here are specific examples of academic/ intellectual depth . . ." ①

_____ "one of my best students in class," "loves learning," "sees relationships between concepts other students miss . . ." ①

_____ "a good deal of intellectual potential," "tries awfully hard," "I see evidence of academic prowess." ②

_____ "Personally, he/she is a good kid," "likable," "completes work on time," "an above average student," "lots of potential for growth." More description of personal—rather than academic—qualities. ③

VIII. Rank Ordering of Admission Strengths. Rank each of the following qualities as they apply to you as a college applicant. For example, if you feel your "test scores" are your strongest feature as viewed by colleges, mark that item with a one (1).

_2_ Coursework (strong, competitive courses)

_1_ Grades

_5_ Academic recommendations

_3_ Rank in class

_8_ Extracurricular activities

_6_ Test scores

_4_ Personal attributes/personality

_7_ Work experiences

_____ Other. What?

_____

IX. Summarize Your Admission Profile. Look at your responses to items I through VIII. Comment on your strengths and weaknesses as a college applicant. In how many areas (I-VIII) do you show the very strongest preparation (strongest is indicated with ①)? What about weaker areas? Can you do anything now to strengthen your preparation?

(some can be renumbered.)
I am very strong in school
I don't have most of my
test scores yet but I can
study more and retake.
I need more e.c.s.

Evaluate Your Admission Profile

What have you learned about yourself as a candidate for admission? How do you assess your readiness for college? What strengths about yourself will you want to emphasize in the admission process? What weaknesses will you need to take into consideration?

Next, share your responses on Worksheets 2 and 4 with your parents, your college counselor and/or a good friend. How do they react? Do they have any additions or comments about any of your answers? Make notes of their comments and additions on the worksheets. Your counselor will help you analyze what your responses to these worksheets say about your college choices. Regularly update Worksheet 3 with any new activities, work experiences or awards.

Sometimes learning about yourself can be painful because your sense of yourself may not be what you wish it were or hope it will become. You may have found you are not as strong a college applicant as you thought you were. But keep in mind the essential message of Chapter 1—there are many colleges from which to choose, and your happiness and your comfort in *the* right educational environment is what is most important. In life, each of us deals with the reality of our situation and with the knowledge of our strengths and weaknesses. As you progress through the admission process, keep your strengths in mind but also let your weaknesses serve as a source of direction for improvement. It is not what you are today that is the most important—it is what you will become after your undergraduate years that is most meaningful to a fulfilling professional career and a happy life.

Using the knowledge you have gained about yourself in this chapter, you can now identify the qualities that will make a college a good match for you. That is the purpose of Chapter 3.

CHAPTER 3

■■■■■■■■■■■■■■■■■■■■■

WHAT ARE YOU LOOKING
FOR IN A COLLEGE?

Of all the chapters in the book, this one is perhaps the most important. Here, you will discover those qualities or characteristics that make a particular college a good fit or match for you. Chapter 2 was about you. It allowed you to assess yourself on a number of traits which are pertinent to your college planning. Now, armed with that information, you are asked to learn a bit about some of the characteristics of colleges that make them special. Once you have named and identified your preferences, you will be able, in Chapter 4, to list colleges that are right for you.

When you finish this chapter, you will have an answer to the question: What am I looking for in a college? After reading this chapter, you will have considered a number of qualities found in colleges and universities: size, location, admission difficulty, academic offerings, and so forth. Each is explained in terms of how it might affect your college experience. So, as you read about each characteristic, think about yourself and your preferences. If, for example, you have trouble identifying your own preferences for size of college, after reading about that characteristic, reflect on yourself and your school experiences so far. What is the size of your high school? Have you felt comfortable there? Have you ever attended a smaller or larger school? How did that feel?

The key to using this chapter well is to answer the questions honestly and thoroughly. Try not to anticipate how your parents or friends would want you to respond. Answer for yourself. Students usually know what they prefer and where they will do well.

Maybe you are wondering why these college qualities are even important since you simply want the "best" college you can get into. But, wait a minute! "Best" means what is ideal for you, not what is best in some generic sense. The right approach to finding a college is to identify the characteristics that fit you and will make for four successful, happy and productive years. Yes, it will be time consuming to think about the qualities colleges offer, but such an analysis yields better college options. Regardless of the college you select, you will know *why* you have selected that particular school, and knowing why you have made a choice is perhaps one of the most important skills you can develop. Also, remember, that what is "best" for one student may not be "best" for another student. The only way to determine the "best" college for you is by thinking about all the different features found in colleges as described in this chapter.

As you progress through this chapter, remember there are no easy answers or correct responses to questions about the right size college for you, the right location, or the right academic environment. You might be successful in a range of college sizes, locations, and academic environments. But in some environments you might thrive as a student, while, in others, you might find barriers to your success. Completing Worksheet 5 will help you build your ideal college profile. Pinpointing these qualities, in turn, will lead you to a list of colleges that are right for you. Remember also that this is the beginning of your college search. What you seek in a college may change over the months. This worksheet starts the process of thinking and learning about characteristics that distinguish one college from the next.

Proceed methodically through the worksheet. Allow an hour or so for the task. First, read the description of each quality carefully. Then think about how that quality relates to you as a person and as a potential college student. Finally, complete the questions asked of you about each quality.

After you have finish Worksheet 5, proceed to Worksheet 6—a summary of the characteristics you are looking for in a college. Completing it will give you an overview of college features that will lead to your academic and social success. In Chapter 4, you will identify, then compare, the colleges that meet your now established criteria.

Worksheet 5—Qualities That Will Make a College Right for You

When you see numbers from 1 to 5 sandwiched between two statements, circle the number which best reflects your level of preference. Circle 1 if you have a strong preference for the quality listed on the left. Circle 5 if you have a strong preference for the quality listed on the right. Use 2, 3 or 4 to reflect varying levels of preference.

Quality 1—Size

Colleges vary in size from under 100 to over 60,000 students. Think carefully about which size is best for you both academically and socially. The following considerations may help you:

Smaller colleges provide students with many benefits. First, they can be just as diverse, fun and interesting as larger schools. Students talk about the range of opportunities and the depth of their friendships at smaller schools. Second, classes are more intimate than those at large universities, which allows for greater interaction between student and professor. You'll have more opportunities to contribute in class and it's likely you'll really know your professors. By knowing your professors, you can benefit from their expertise and they can help you with any academic weak points. Further, they will be able to write you knowledgeable recommendations for jobs or graduate schools. Smaller colleges are best if you prefer discussion classes (where you are a participant) as opposed to lecture classes (where the teacher does most of the talking). You are also more likely to be able to register for the classes you desire.

In addition, smaller colleges tend to place greater emphasis on personal development. In other words, it's easier for students to learn about themselves: their interests, abilities, and possible career paths. The best preparation for someone who is unsure of his or her career direction is a liberal arts and sciences curriculum found at most small colleges. At smaller colleges, teaching is usually the top priority of faculty members—research may be less important. This emphasis may mean more exciting classroom experiences (which often result in increased understanding and higher grades). At larger universities, in contrast, you may be taught by graduate students, not professors.

Smaller colleges provide greater opportunities to participate in extracurricular activities because you don't have to be a superstar to get involved. At smaller colleges, you experience less competition for the use of academic facilities such as library resources and specialized equipment. Also, you usually experience a great sense of community. Because it is difficult to get "lost," small colleges often facilitate the development of student confidence. Don't discount the advantages of being a significant fish in a small pond—it can do wonders for your self-esteem and sense of accomplishment.

Larger colleges also present students with many benefits. You will notice great range and variety in the courses offered at large schools. You may be able to explore (and perhaps take classes in) two different fields of study— for example, arts and sciences and engineering. Also, students who are very undecided about the subjects they want to study may feel that large universities (with many strong majors) will be the safest educational choice. Special advanced facilities and equipment are available at many large universities. At large universities, students invariably find more activities from which to choose. Significantly, nationally known and popular sports teams increases a school's name recognition. Further, many students prefer the anonymity a large school offers. Additionally, some students prefer lecture classes to those that are more discussion-oriented.

Size considerations often cause students to limit the field of potential colleges too early in the process of choosing a college. Students who reject larger colleges should remember that some larger universities are more personal than others. Some large universities provide personal attention, such as individual academic advisors. Students from large high schools often say they don't want to attend a college smaller than their high school. Others feel they will miss a fun college life if they attend a smaller college. Remember, smaller colleges can be just as diverse and just as fun and they can provide good career preparation. Also remember, over 80% of private colleges in the U.S.—and almost a quarter of public colleges—have enrollments of under 2,500. So don't limit yourself based on false assumptions about size.

High desire for accessible teachers	1	(2)	3	4	5	Low desire for accessible teachers
I would likely get better grades in small classes	1	2	3	(4)	5	I would likely get similar grades in small or large classes
More discussion-oriented classes	1	2	(3)	4	5	More lecture-oriented classes
I learn best discussing ideas/interacting with the instructor and other students	1	(2)	3	4	5	I learn best by reading/listening/taking notes
Desire for tutors/extra assistance	1	(2)	3	4	5	No desire for tutors/extra assistance
A close-knit, family-like environment	1	2	(3)	4	5	A place where I can blend in with the crowd

First, look at the following size distinctions:
    Small size—under 3,000 students
    Medium size—between 3,000 and 10,000 students
    Large size—between 10,000 and 20,000 students
    Largest size—over 20,000 students
(Note: These size distinctions are arbitrary and intended merely to assist you in considering general size parameters.)

Second, on the basis of the discussion and your circled responses above, check those sizes that you feel are best for you:

_____ Small   ☒ Medium   ☒ Large _____ Largest

Any comments/further thoughts about the size of your ideal college?:

Don't want too small or too big

Quality 2—Academic Environment

Academic environment includes your priority on academics, the academic pressure that is right for you, and the learning resources you need.

Naturally, since college is an academic undertaking, classes and other "academic things" make up the bulk of your collegiate experience. Finding the appropriate level of academic challenge is important to your choice of colleges. Think about how much academic challenge is right for you. Do you want a college where you must work hard and study hard, or would you prefer one where you could earn respectable grades without knocking yourself out? Think carefully about how much time you want to spend on academic pursuits in college. If you truly enjoy talking about ideas and intellectual subjects, you may desire a more "academic" atmosphere in your college choice.

Also, think here about your response to academic pressure and to competition from others. Are you at home with a tremendous workload? Do you prioritize well? Can you discipline yourself? If your answers to these questions are yes, you should select a vigorous academic environment. If, however, you prefer to perform consistently at the top of your class, if you become distraught with a grade lower than an A, or if you don't work well under stress, you may respond better in a college with normal academic pressure.

Priority on Academics

Very intellectual/   1   2   3   4   (5)   Balance between
scholarly emphasis   intellectual/social
                                                        sides of campus life

Academic Pressure

Ready/able to   1   2   (3)   4   5   Ready/able to
handle the most   handle normal
vigorous academic   academic pressure
environment

Learning Resources

I need/want learning   1   (2)   3   4   5   I have no need for
resources such as a   these learning
learning center, tutors,   resources
extra time on tests, etc.

Other Academic/Curricular Qualities

In addition to offering certain concentrated areas of potential study (majors), colleges vary in terms of other academic qualities. Would you enjoy more freedom or more structure insofar as courses you are required to take? Would work experiences, internships or the availability of independent study enhance your academic success? Would you like a particularly strong study abroad experience? Do you want to prepare for the military? Many academic variables are listed below. Check *any* that you would like in your college.

- ✓ internships/work experiences
- ✓ considerable freedom in choosing courses
- _____ programs for students with learning style differences (LD, ADD, ADHD, etc.)
- _____ independent study options
- _____ applying what I learn to real world problems
- _____ preparation for the military
- ✓ more hands-on learning opportunities
- ✓ counseling/psychological/medical services
- ✓ courses geared to my specific academic/career interests
- _____ excellent study abroad programs
- _____ research opportunities
- ✓ personalized academic advising
- ✓ personalized career advising
- _____ writing center

Is there anything else related to the academic environment that is important to you? If so, describe it here:

_____

_____

_____

Quality 3—Academic Offerings

This category refers to your potential college major and not your potential career. It's important for you to keep that distinction in mind. A major is a subject you enjoy and would like to study in college. Refer to Appendix D for a list of major fields. Do you enjoy English or history? Does math or communication sound interesting?

Notice the continuum below between "A liberal arts and sciences college is best" and "A college that will prepare me for a specific career after four years of college is best." Liberal arts and sciences is the term used to describe the most general and most common form of undergraduate education in the U.S. It includes the humanities (English, languages, music, art, philosophy, etc.), the social sciences (psychology, history, political science, etc.) and the "hard" sciences (biology, mathematics, geology, etc.). The liberal arts and sciences often serve as a springboard for future study (for example, graduate school, law school, medical school or business school) and for the world of work. If you are uncertain as to a career, then you should select liberal arts and sciences. On the other hand, you may want to take more courses in an area of interest. Career-oriented schools have classes that more directly relate to careers in such areas as engineering, business, physical therapy or architecture upon completion of your undergraduate degree.

It is perfectly OK not to know what your ultimate career will be. Most high school students do not know. In fact, coming to the wrong conclusion too early about a career is worse than not knowing. Most high school students have not been exposed to many career alternatives, making a final career decision premature. The undergraduate years can be a time of discovery about yourself and your career goals. If, however, you feel confident in your selection of a career goal and want a college that offers your particular program, enter the name of your program below.

| A liberal arts and sciences college is best | 1 | 2 | 3 | 4 | 5 | A college that will prepare me for a specific career after four years of college is best |

I want a broad-based (1) 2 3 4 5 I would like to focus
education so as to on classes that are
consider several careers relevant to my current
career interests

What subjects would you like to learn more about? And/or which subjects will you consider as a major? (Some colleges allow you to have more than one major.) You might want to look at the list provided in Appendix D.

Human mind / body interactions

What career(s) have you considered? If none, say so.

none

Quality 4—Cost/Availability of Financial Aid

Costs vary greatly from one college to another. Many students, however, make too many assumptions about cost too early in the process of choosing a college. There are many forms of financial aid available. While most aid is given (naturally) to those who can demonstrate need (by the results of a standardized financial aid analysis using forms such as the Free Application for Federal Student Aid), aid is also available for students who have achieved academic excellence or those with special abilities.

Perhaps no factor in college selection is as potentially limiting as cost. There are so many myths associated with cost. Students and families may believe that little money is available, that only poverty-stricken families receive aid or that students need to be super scholars to get money from colleges. The truth is that enormous resources are available for families who take the time to explore financial aid opportunities. The reference section of this book provides a starting list of places to get information about college costs and financial aid. For example, the publisher of this book, Octameron Associates, is a leading authority on college costs and financial aid. Their books are relatively inexpensive and up-to-date.

Below, indicate the extent to which cost/availability of aid is a consideration in your choice of a college. It is important to talk this over with your family.

Cost is a major factor 1 2 (3) 4 5 Cost is a minor factor
in choosing a college in choosing a college

| I need to do a thorough search of financial aid options | 1 | (2) | 3 | 4 | 5 | No search of financial aid options is necessary |

| Cost will lead me to an in-state college... or to one that costs less... or to one where I can get a scholarship | 1 | 2 | (3) | 4 | 5 | Cost will not lead me in these directions |

Comments about cost/financial aid in your college search:

I really need to try for scholarships.

Quality 5—Religion

The extent of religious influence varies from college to college. Some colleges are related to a particular denomination, but are not governed or influenced by the church; these schools tend to have very little religious influence. On the other hand, there are Christian colleges, for example, that have far closer relationships that extend to required religion classes and/or religious practices (such as chapel services).

Regardless of the extent of religious life, you might desire a college where many, if not most, of the students belong to your religion. Is this factor important to you in selecting a college?

| Religious life is an important factor in choosing a college | 1 | 2 | 3 | 4 | (5) | Religious life is not a factor in choosing a college |

| I want a college where religious life is emphasized | 1 | 2 | 3 | (4) | 5 | No emphasis on religious life |

| I'd like to be at a college with many students who share my religious background | 1 | 2 | 3 | 4 | (5) | Having many students who share my religious background is not a significant college planning variable |

Comments about religious influence:

_____None_____

_____

Quality 6—Ethnicity

Hispanic/Latino, American Indian, Asian, and African-American students benefit in many ways by attending a college with a high number of students who belong to the same ethnic group. For example, for the African-American student, predominantly Black colleges offer students the opportunity to interact with Black role models, to develop a "network" of contacts that can be helpful in getting jobs, and to learn in a comfortable environment. Many respected leaders in government, education and the professions are graduates of these institutions. Similarly, students who might feel isolated on predominantly "white" campuses often benefit from the camaraderie and closeness that is possible by being with others who share their heritage.

Would the presence of other students who represent your heritage foster your sense of belonging? Would you feel like an outcast if you were one of only a few students representing your ethnic background? Would you like specialized programs for minority students??

It's important that I   1 2 3 (4) 5 It's unimportant that
attend a college where   I attend a college
there are many students   where there are many
who share my ethnic/racial   students who share
heritage   my heritage

Comments about racial/ethnic issues in my choice of college:

_____

_____

Quality 7—Coeducation Or Single Sex

This consideration is predominately for women, although there are some fine all-male colleges as well. Don't be too hasty here. Both women's and men's colleges offer special educational advantages and ought to be considered very carefully. For example, several studies have found that students at women's colleges become more academically involved in classes, are more likely to pursue advanced degrees, and show more intellectual self-esteem when compared with their counterparts in coeducational institutions. Further, a women's college gives women more opportunities for academic success in an environment where they don't need to compete with men for both classroom time and positions of campus leadership. Women's colleges are just as fun, just as interesting, and, in many ways, can be just as "real world" as coed schools.

What kind of school would you *consider?*

___X___ Coed ____ Men ____ Women

Quality 8—Student Body Characteristics

Identifying the characteristics about students with whom you will feel most at home can be meaningful as you contemplate your college choices.

Think about the traits of the students attending a college that is a good match for you. Below is a list of words and phrases that describe students. Look over the list. Keep in mind that most colleges enroll a wide variety of students. What you are doing here is highlighting the personality characteristics and the values of students at a college that is a good match for you.

First, circle any quality that describes the types of student with whom you would enjoy going to school. In the blanks provided, list any other characteristics that you would like to find in your future classmates.

adventurous	aggressive	ambitious	artsy
athletic	balanced	career oriented	caring
compassionate	conservative	cosmopolitan	creative
diverse	down-to-earth	dress-conscious	energetic
focused	friendly	fun	good values
idealistic	independent	innovative	involved
laid back	lawful	liberal	moral
motivated	nonjudgmental	open	opinionated
outdoorsy	patient	politically-active	practical
realistic	respectful	risk taking	scholarly
sensitive	serious	social	spirited
spontaneous	supportive	tightly-knit	tolerant
traditional	unconventional	understanding	
interested in cultural activities		interested in learning for the sake of learning	

_____   _____

_____   _____

_____   _____

Second, if you circled more than 5 qualities, go back and put a check mark next to the 5 most important ones.

Finally, take a look at the following continuum. Students at the colleges on the left side are traditional; in other words, they are like students you'd find on most campuses. Students at the colleges on the right side are more alternative, free spirited, and independent-minded. The distinction here is arbitrary (and involves generalizing) but your response can be helpful in thinking about broad categories of students at your ideal college. If you can't decide, or if this variable is unimportant, or if you could fit into either side, circle 3.

A more traditional student body is best for me	1 2 ③ 4 5	An alternative, free-spirited, independent-minded student body is best for me

Comments about the students at your ideal college:

I am open to anything pretty much.

Quality 9—Student Life

Colleges are unique in many ways. Some of these differences relate to student life. First, check any of the following that are important to you. Second, list *any* other factors that come to mind.

_____ most students live on-campus

_____ lots of spectator sports

_____ an environmentally active student body

_____ going to athletic games is a big social event

_____ lots of students participate in intramural sports

_____ fraternities/sororities are available

_____ specialized programs for women/gay/multicultural students

__X__ lots of weekend activities

__X__ the food is good

__X__ a safe campus

__X__ a beautiful campus

_____ ramps/easy access to buildings

_____ many leadership opportunities available

__X__ nice residence halls/living spaces

__X__ where a sense of community exists

_____ where I'm recognized for accomplishments outside of class

_____ where I don't feel like a number

_____ community service/volunteer opportunities

_____ very spirited

Are there other characteristics of student life that will make your college experience a better one? If so, list them here:

_____

_____

Quality 10—Activities (Including Athletics)

You may desire a normal variety of activities or you may be looking for a college that offers some specific activity. You might want to continue a high school activity or you might want to develop new interests. Would you like to participate in sports? Which ones? At the varsity, club or intramural level? Do you want to be a leader and/or develop your leadership skills? Are you looking for theater or art or music involvements? Are there other clubs or organizations you would enjoy joining in such areas as religion, international students, outdoor/recreation, community service, ethnic/culture, political, or academic?

Refer to Appendix E for a listing of potential college activities. List those activities of interest to you here:

maybe some intramural

sports w/ friends

maybe clubs where I

can learn new things

Quality 11—Big Name School or Best Fit School?

Students vary in the priority they place on attending a well-known college or university. Students who want to attend a "name" college or university sometimes put that desire above other factors in choosing a college. These students may be less concerned with the overall fit of the college. "Fit" or "match" refers to all factors or qualities that a college possesses such as size, programs offered, characteristics of the students, quality of faculty, location, and so forth. In other words, "fit" takes a broad view of college planning criteria.

It's perfectly OK for an "A" student to want to attend an excellent quality college. But remember that dozens and dozens of colleges have superior professors, outstanding academic facilities, and a high percentage of graduates admitted to top graduate schools. And most colleges have excellent networking possibilities after graduation. Further, other factors beyond academic prestige are also important, such as your happiness and your success!

Thus, both name and fit may be important to you. But, given the separation between "name" and "fit" as described here, where would you put yourself on the following continuum? Remember, your position may change, but where would you rate yourself on this factor today?

| The "name" or the "prestige" of a college is most important in my college search | 1 | 2 | 3 | (4) | 5 | The fit of the college for me (size, social and academic atmosphere, etc.) is most important in my college search |

Quality 12—Admission Difficulty

Consider what you have learned about yourself in Chapter 2. Being realistic is very important here. Consider the level of difficulty of your courses, your curiosity, independence and organization. Review the results of Your Admission Profile, Worksheet 4. Also, think about how you compare with others in your own high school graduating class. What level of admission difficulty do you feel you fit into?

| The most selective colleges are appropriate for me | 1 | (2) | 3 | 4 | 5 | Less selective colleges are appropriate for me |

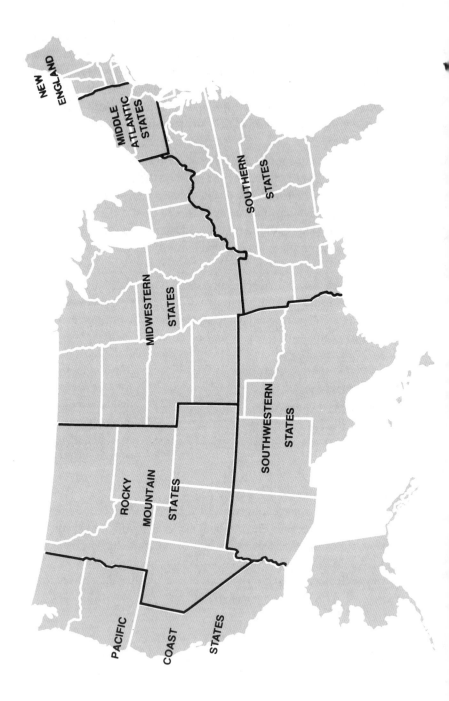

NEW ENGLAND

MIDDLE ATLANTIC STATES

SOUTHERN STATES

MIDWESTERN STATES

SOUTHWESTERN STATES

ROCKY MOUNTAIN STATES

PACIFIC COAST STATES

Quality 13—Location

The first task here is to decide the relative weight of location in your college selection. Is location more important than other factors such as over-all quality of the college, its academic offerings, size or cost? Or is location relatively low on your college-choosing priority list? Do you want to attend school close to home? Will you want to come home often (even the least homesick come home occasionally)?

Location is the most important factor in choosing a college	1	② 3	4	5	Other factors are more important in choosing a college
I'd like a college close to home	1	② 3	4	5	Closeness to home is not particularly important to me

Think about the following in regard to the location of your college:

Regions of the country where you would prefer to go to college

Are some parts of the country more appealing than others? Give thought as well to the importance that you or your parents might attach to the ease and expense of traveling to the college. Do you have relatives or close friends in particular states that you would like to be near? (A relative or friend can be a valuable support system when you're away from home for the first time.) Do you prefer certain types of climates?

Do, however, keep in mind that you're choosing an academic environment where you will spend four years—you are not choosing a vacation site! First, look carefully at the map on the opposite page. Circle those regions of the country you will consider in choosing a college:

Pacific Coast	Southwestern	Rocky Mountain
New England	Middle Atlantic	Southern
Midwestern		

Specific states in which you would prefer to go to college

Indicate any states which you particularly like. Try not to think of particular colleges within a given state, but rather, of states that you would enjoy going to college in. California

Close to a city?

Consider the following three possibilities:

1. A college in a major city. Being in a medium or large city allows you to take advantage of a number of amenities. If you enjoy major or professional sports teams, or cultural institutions such as art museums or the symphony, a city or suburban college may best satisfy your needs. Will you go crazy if you don't have at least one large shopping mall and several movie theaters within 15 minutes of your dorm? Then this option will be best.

2. A college near a large city, but not in it. These colleges are located on the outskirts of the city or in the suburbs. This option gives students access to a city, but yet a distinct campus "feel" that often includes large, grassy areas.

3. A college in a small town or a rural location. If, however, you prefer a more serene or relaxed college atmosphere, you may be able to study better in a tranquil location such as a rural college in a small college town. Such colleges may be one or two hours or more from a medium to large city. Typically, college towns show great support for college students and their activities. Store owners may call you by name and cash your check without identification. Most of the services (like pizza places, dry cleaners, etc.) in small towns cater to students. Furthermore, colleges further away from a city tend to go to great lengths to bring concerts, speakers and other programs to the campus.

Which of these options sound appealing to you as you think about the kind of place in which you will be comfortable? Check any (or all):

___✓___ 1. In a major city

___✓___ 2. Near a large city, but not in it

_____ 3. In a small town or a rural location (or where the college is the focus of the town)

Any other location preferences? For example, close to outdoor/nature activities (hiking, streams, mountains, kayaking, etc.)? In the downtown of a huge city? Near a beach?

near beach

Quality 14—Academic Success In College

Look carefully at all the factors you've identified as being important to you as you consider colleges that would be right for you. Is there anything else a college could provide to help you accomplish your academic goals and do your best? Indicate any additional factors here. Include whether you have made the decision to go to college by yourself, and/or whether you'd like to consider taking a year off between high school and college.

> I want to go to college
> right out of high school,
> I am ready to start my life.

Quality 15—Fitting In/Being Comfortable In College

Again, look carefully at the factors you have said are important in choosing your college. Are there any other qualities the college could provide which would lead to your overall comfort with your college? Think about this: If you were to visit a college tomorrow, is there anything else you would ask about or look for in addition to those factors you listed on this worksheet? List any additional factors below.

> - availability of classes/
>   closeness w/ professors
> - good area?
> - sense of family/community

Worksheet 6—Characteristics of Your Ideal College

By completing Worksheet 5, you have considered 15 qualities or characteristics important to you in selecting a college. In the spaces below, summarize what you have discovered about the qualities you seek and their importance. More specifically, review your responses to each of the 15 qualities. Select the eight most important features of a college and write statements summarizing what you are looking for in a college. The examples may help you.

Examples:

1. I'm looking for a small college because I seek contact with professors and opportunities to get involved in lots of athletic activities. Size of the college is very important to me.

2. While not imperative, I would prefer a college with many Catholic students.

3. All locations are OK but my preference is for colleges in New England.

4. I'm looking for a liberal arts and sciences college since I'm still deciding on a career.

5. It is very important for me to have a balance between academics and social life. I don't want a pressure-cooker college!

6. I should pay particular attention to colleges which either cost less or where I might be eligible for some type of scholarship.

7. I'd like a college that cares about the environment.

1. _medium size college to have more accessibility to teachers and have a sense of community_

2. safe area (living on or off campus). I like feeling safe.

3. variety of majors b/c I have no idea what I want to do.

4. I really want a good balance between school and social life.

5. I need scholarship availability

6. preferably in southern
california; close enough
but far enough away
from home.

7. I really want a college
where I feel comfortable,
not like everyone is
better than me.

8. coed college is important

CHAPTER 4

■■■■■■■■■■■■■■■■■■■

BUILDING YOUR COLLEGE LIST

Now that you've learned a bit about yourself (Chapter 2) and identified the qualities that will make a college right for you (Chapter 3), the next step is to find out which specific colleges best meet your background and talents, as well as those that come closest to matching the combination of factors you identified as important to your academic and social success. College planning involves three key decision points:

1. which colleges you will consider,
2. which colleges you will apply to, and
3. which college you will attend.

This Chapter is intended to help you with points (1) and (2).

This might all sound a bit overwhelming; after all, you have more than 4,000 colleges to choose from. But by following the suggestions offered in this Chapter, your systematic analysis and review can make the process quite doable. Remember that for every student, there are likely dozens of "good match" colleges. This isn't like hunting for the rare pearl in the oyster. Rather, in college planning, pearls are everywhere. They are just waiting for you to find them.

Arriving at Your Initial List of Colleges

Without knowing you or your goals, background, and interests, we cannot present you with a list of specific colleges to which you should apply. We can, however, give you a plan for finding those colleges. That plan follows.

NOTE #1: Your personal visits to colleges are a good source of information at various stages of your list building process. Campus visits are not discussed here because Chapter 5 is devoted to this topic.

NOTE #2: Please remember that books go out of print and, more likely, links to materials on the Internet change. Many books and websites are provided in this Chapter in the hope that if one source of material is not available, another may be.

List-Building Strategies

Deciding on colleges to apply to takes time, patience, research skill, and determination. At the end of this section, you will list 20 colleges that seem right for you. There are eleven strategies mentioned here. Not all of them will be applicable to your search and you may decide to do them in a different order. Thus, how you arrive at this list depends on a number of factors, but here are some general "list-building" strategies.

1. Speak to your counselor about your needs and interests, and request a list of colleges to check out. High school counselors are, for most students, the key resource people in providing information about colleges. You should meet with your counselor as often as your school suggests and your needs dictate. Give your counselor as much information about yourself as necessary to enable him or her to recommend colleges that are right for you. Share your goals for college and your dreams for the future. Show your counselor the Worksheets you completed in this book. Remember, however, that counselors are busy people, often with many different responsibilities. So be organized when you visit with your counselor—be prepared with questions and issues for discussion.

2. Go online and complete one or more of the college searches available. For example, the major college planning websites (collegeboard.com, princetonreview.com, usnews.com) provide ways of inputting your wants and then retrieving a list of potential colleges. These types of computerized searches may be available in your high school. To search for colleges, you enter the basic facts that are relevant in finding a college (such as major, location, or size) and the search returns a list of colleges that meet the criteria you have set. While this is a good first step, these approaches are limited, as the program doesn't know you, and therefore is unable to determine college environments that are appropriate for you.

3. Investigate your high school counseling/career office. There may be other materials available in your high school counseling office such as books, online resources, DVDs, tapes, videos, podcasts, and computer programs that can help. Most high schools have libraries for students to use. Some have comprehensive college planning tools such as Naviance. Many college admission officers visit high schools and you should check to see when these visits are scheduled.

4. Use book retailers such as Amazon or Barnes & Noble to find general or specialized books on colleges. You'll find guidebooks on an array of topics. There are also books available for those seeking informa-

tion about a variety of academic and career fields such as visual and performing arts, journalism, and creative writing.

5. Use the Internet for specialized research. For example, to find out which colleges do not require entrance tests, look at fairtest.org. And to learn which colleges require SAT Subject Tests visit compassprep.com/admissions_req_subjects.aspx. For descriptions of clusters of colleges (often these are small, liberal arts schools), explore Colleges of Distinction (collegesofdistinction.com), Colleges That Change Lives (ctcl.com), and Council on Public Liberal Arts Colleges (coplac.org). To locate college geographically, check out Professor Pathfinder's U.S. College and Universities Map (hedbergmaps.com) and The College Atlas and Planner (Wintergreen-Orchard House). If you are seeking a college with a religious affiliation, *The College Handbook* carries a complete listing. Finally, there are niche websites—ldanatl.org, wrightslaw.com, and ldonline.org would all be useful for students with learning disabilities.

6. Talk to your parents. They may have perspectives about schools they attended or know about. Further, they may have heard comments from friends or relatives which, when combined with other sources of information, can be helpful in choosing your college. On the other hand, some adults will stereotype colleges as "a party school," "a school for nerds," "not a 'good' school," etc. Listen to their perceptions, but do your own research as well.

7. Talk to your friends. Ask the ones who have just been through the college admission process for their impressions on colleges they are considering or attending. They may have recently visited a number of colleges and can share their impressions. Their own research, their own impressions, and their own travels may be useful to you. Also, stay tuned to the "college grapevine" at your school or among your friends, but with this word of caution: nobody knows your background and your feelings as well as you do. So, listen attentively, but reserve final judgment until you investigate for yourself. Remember, one person's ideal college can be another person's collegiate disaster.

8. There are also professionals trained in the area of college admission planning. These people, called educational consultants, assist students in choosing a college. Consultants combine knowledge about colleges (gained, in part, by traveling to dozens of colleges annually) with the time necessary to be able to explore your situation in depth. You should ask about their membership in professional organizations and

the credentials the consultant possesses. For a listing of Educational Consultants, contact the Independent Educational Consultants Association (IECA), IECAonline.com, the Higher Education Consultants Association (HECA), hecaonline.com, and the National Association for College Admission Counseling (NACAC), nacacnet.org. Further, you might ask if the consultant is a "Certified Educational Planner." You can find information about this credential at aicep.org.

9. Read broadly and become acquainted with colleges and college admission in the twenty-first century. For example, scan some of the general college planning books such as *Getting into the Right College* by Fiske and Hammond, *Admission Matters* by Springer and Franck and *Less Stress, More Success* by Jones, Ginsburg and Jablow. "How Admissions Works" (howstuffworks.com/college-admission.htm) is a primer on college admission. There are a few authors who offer great insight into the college admission process and are highly respected in the field. One is Loren Pope, author of *Colleges That Change Lives* and *Looking Beyond The Ivy League*. *The Gatekeepers* by Jacques Steinberg is a good source of information about selective college admission, and a reliable book on the college search process is *Harvard Schmarvard* by Jay Mathews. *The College Finder* (by this author) is a book of lists of colleges in categories such as "Colleges with excellent programs in biology," Colleges with great study abroad programs," and "Colleges where students with learning disabilities succeed." Education Conservancy (educationconservancy.org) offers a healthy approach to college planning.

10. Start thinking about possible majors. You can check a resource such as *The College Board Book of Majors* for listings on colleges that offer certain academic programs. In addition, you can google the name of your proposed major. Further, here are some websites worth checking out: dowhatyouare.com, careerkey.org, keirsey.com, mappingyourfuture.org, typelogic.com, knowyourtype.com, mymajors.com (links to information on majors), and careers.siue.edu/majors/majors/default.html.

11. Start thinking about possible careers. As we have said elsewhere in this book, to find a "good match" college, you do not need to know exactly what you will be when you grow up. Indeed, the process of career formulation takes time and experience and often develops as one moves through the college years. On the other hand, getting help exploring interests and potential careers is wise for most students. The more options you consider, the more likely you will make the best

ultimate career choice. As such, high school students benefit from taking a career inventory or gathering vocational information through research. Several career-oriented books are listed in the Resources for College Planning. Some helpful websites are: collegetoolkit.com, careercruising.com and strengthfinder.com.

Finally, here are a few other ways of arriving at your list of colleges:

If you are interested in particular states, go to one of the "review" guidebooks (for example, *Fiske Guide to Colleges*) and read the descriptions of the colleges within that state. (Of course, these guides only describe a fraction of colleges in each state, but it is a beginning.)

If you have a few colleges in mind (say, one your sister or a friend attends), read about each college in one of the subjective guides. Using *The Insider's Guide to Colleges* or *Fiske Guide to Colleges*, look at a few schools you are interested in and then look at "Overlap Schools." In other words, students who applied to such and such college also applied to these other colleges. This can help expand your initial list.

Incorporating Your Personal Criteria Into the Search

As you go through the process of arriving at your list of colleges, make sure to incorporate your personal search criteria into the search. Review Worksheets 5 and 6 to identify the factors you listed as important. On Worksheet 6, you listed the eight characteristics of your ideal college. Each of these represents one dimension of your search. One might have to do with size or location. One might relate to religious preference, academic interest, or some other factor. These are the building blocks upon which your list of colleges is based. Now use some of the methods described above to find colleges that meet your personal criteria. For example:

If you are looking mainly in-state, you will want to review descriptions on websites and in books such as *The College Handbook* for information about the school, its admission policies, and other qualities. You may be able to visit some of these colleges.

If you are seeking a Catholic college and would like to be on the West coast, use any of the guidebooks mentioned in this Chapter (or do an online search for Catholic colleges) to identify Catholic schools in California, Oregon, Washington, and other states you are considering. www.ncaa.org and look at colleges sorted by conference. Or use the Wintergreen/Orchard House *Index of Majors and Sports*.

For African American students, look at blackexcel.org and ed.gov/about/inits/list/whhcu/edlite. Hispanic/Latino students might look at hacu.net.

If you want a Division III women's lacrosse program, go to a site such as ncaa.com and look at colleges sorted by conference. Or use the Wintergreen/Orchard House *Index of Majors and Sports*.

If security on campus is one of your top concerns, look at sites such as ope.ed.gov/security or securityoncampus.org.

Good advice on costs is found in Leider's *Don't Miss Out* and Cassidy's *The Scholarship Book*.

If you want to try for a merit-based scholarship, look at *The A's and B's of Academic Scholarships* (published by Octameron Associates).

The National Association of Independent Colleges and Universities has a website with valuable information about colleges in their network: ucan-network.org.

After you have talked to your advisor and used the resources and ideas described in this chapter, you should have an initial list of colleges. List the names of colleges you have chosen on Worksheet 7. This is your potential college list. Your list may be as small as 5 or as large as 40 (20 spaces are provided). Whatever the size of the list, this is where your research and comparisons of colleges begin.

If you haven't already done so, e-mail or write each of these colleges asking for information. As you decide on which 20 or so schools to include, think about two components:

1. The Academic Factors: Where am I going to be pushed, not shoved? Where am I going to be able to get the best grades? Where is the learning environment that best fits my own learning style?

2. The Social Factors: Where am I going to be comfortable? Where will I fit in? Where will I have lots of friends?

Final Advice

As you come up with your list:

- Do not focus too much on major.
- Do not focus too much on cost.
- Do not focus too much on location.
- Do not focus too much on prestige.

Carefully consider important issues, but don't neglect others. For example, say cost is a primary concern. Look for colleges that meet the financial needs of its students. Look for colleges that offer a lot of merit scholarships (most of that information is available on the web), and look at schools that are just as good, but cost less. So, yes, look at all of these financial factors, but also keep in mind other factors, like location, size, and the characteristics of students, as you arrive at the list of colleges you are considering.

Worksheet 7—Colleges You Are Considering

Name of College   **Name of College**

1. LMU   11. UCLA
2. UCSB   12. U of Col. @ Denver
3. Pepperdine   13. National University
4. Azusa Pacific   14. UCSC
5. Chapman   15. U of Oregon
6. U of San Diego   16. UCD
7. U of Redlands   17. Biola U
8. PLNU   18. U of Pacific
9. UCSD   19.
10. Santa Clara U   20.

Comparing Your College Choices

Worksheet 7 lists schools that have made the "first cut" and you want to learn more about them. The next step involves researching your options with the goal of arriving at the final list of colleges to which you will apply. In this section, we will outline a general approach to researching colleges. Your specific approach will vary with the resources available to you, the time you want to take to do this work, and the individual factors important to you in your college search.

As you begin your search, be wary of out-of-date or questionable sources of college information. Seek people who know what is currently happening on a college campus. Popular magazine articles listing the "Best Colleges" are unreliable because no completely objective criterion exists for rating colleges. Further, only you and your advisors know what is best for you.

At this point, your goal is not to select the one college you feel best about. It is to begin to differentiate the colleges knowledgeably and narrow your list to those colleges where you will apply for admission.

Use the tools mentioned in this Chapter to research each of the colleges you listed on Worksheet 7. Worksheet 8 (College Fact Finder) provides spaces for you to fill in the results of your research. There are four forms provided. If you are researching more than twelve colleges, make copies of this Worksheet. Let's look at the components:

—You are asked to indicate where the college is located and how you will get there. For example, is it within driving distance? Will you be able to take a non-stop flight?

—In the next space, you will write down the number of students enrolled.

—Note whether the college offers the academic programs you seek. Remember, however, that you don't need to know exactly what your career will be. You are looking for an academic environment in which to grow and learn about your career options. If you don't have a specific career in mind, comment on whether the college seems like a good place to explore. For example, does it seem easy to change majors? Are graduates getting jobs in a wide variety of fields?

—The space provided for your comments about "Life outside of class" is important and will be discussed separately below.

—You are asked to list one positive and one negative feature about the college. All colleges have both!

—You are also asked whether the college is a high-, medium-, or low-chance-of-admission school for you. The discussion that begins on page 89 provides guidelines to use for determining your likelihood of admission.

—Cost is found in most guidebooks and on the website for each college. Be sure you get comparable data (including room and board, fees, etc.) for each school.

—Use the last space to describe anything else that you find about the college. That "something else" might be sports available, religious or ethnic considerations, merit scholarship opportunities, or any other factor you feel is important to remember about the college.

—At the end of your review, give the college an overall grade. This grade is based on your evaluation of how well the college fits the criteria you have established in Worksheet 6. Don't stress about this grade. It's simply your first impression based on your research.

Completing Worksheet Eight

Now you have a list of colleges and you have forms to use to find out about your college choices. The steps to complete Worksheet 8 are presented next.

Review Guidebooks

Start with one or two of the following guidebooks: *Fiske Guide to Colleges*, *The Insider's Guide to the Colleges*, *Students' Guide to Colleges*, or *The Princeton Review's Best Colleges*. These subjective guidebooks give a few pages of narrative about each college. They are subjective in that they offer reviews of the total environment of the college. These guidebooks evaluate the quality of student life, the academic strengths and weaknesses, and the influence of the location on the nature of campus life. Even though you are using one or more of these books as your initial way to review colleges, remember that the review is not speaking for every student at each college; in fact, some students would disagree completely with the description listed for their own college. Indeed, experts on colleges may also disagree—sometimes fervently—with certain descriptions.

If you have colleges on Worksheet 7 that are not included in one of the subjective guidebooks (a very common occurrence as these books review less than 10% of colleges), use one of the phone book-sized guidebooks, such as *College Board's College Handbook*, *Peterson's Four-Year Colleges*, and *Barron's Profiles of American Colleges*, or the comprehensive websites such as act.org, collegeboard.com, petersons.com, princetonreview.com, or usnews.com. These books and sites provide basic information about colleges, and give such information as academic programs available, general requirements for admission, and cost of attendance. In addition, you might look at *Barron's Best Buys in Higher Education* because it includes reviews of colleges that are not covered in many of the other guidebooks

Worksheet 8—College Fact Finder

COLLEGE NAME	University of Redlands	LMU ✗	UCSB
City & State Distance from a major city? How will I get there?	Redlands, CA	LA, marina del Ray	Santa Barbara
Number of students enrolled?	3,002	5,951	19,186
Does the college offer the academic programs (majors) I'm seeking? If undecided, what programs does the college offer that I'm interested in?			
Life outside of class—Does it seem like an interesting place to be? What features (activities, traditions, location) pertaining to the student experience sound appealing?	seems like stuff to do.	Lots of activities, very active	-bike Highway -very close to beach
What is one positive feature about this college? One negative feature?	-$ aid =NOT Near Beach	-nice area, safe - hilly	↓
Are my admission chances high, medium or low?	high	medium	medium
What is the cost?	$35,240	37,825	11,713
Use this space for notes about this college. Is there anything else you would like to know about the school?	special ($) scholars programs	really like feeling	closer to home
Grade the school, A to F, on the basis of a good match for you.			

Worksheet 8—College Fact Finder

COLLEGE NAME	chapman	USC	USD
City & State Distance from a major city? How will I get there?	orange, CA	LA, CA	san Diego
Number of students enrolled?	4,910	17380	5368
Does the college offer the academic programs (majors) I'm seeking? If undecided, what programs does the college offer that I'm interested in?			
Life outside of class— Does it seem like an interesting place to be? What features (activities, traditions, location) pertaining to the student experience sound appealing?	outdoorsy	tons of activities	
What is one positive feature about this college? One negative feature?	-small -not really by beach	-resources = good big=bad	medium size=good far away = bad
Are my admission chances high, medium or low?	medium	low	medium
What is the cost?	39,200	42818	38,528
Use this space for notes about this college. Is there anything else you would like to know about the school?			
Grade the school, A to F, on the basis of a good match for you.			

Worksheet 8—College Fact Finder

COLLEGE NAME	UCSD	SCU	UCLA
City & State Distance from a major city? How will I get there?	La Jolla	Santa Clara	LA
Number of students enrolled?	23663	5107	26162
Does the college offer the academic programs (majors) I'm seeking? If undecided, what programs does the college offer that I'm interested in?			
Life outside of class— Does it seem like an interesting place to be? What features (activities, traditions, location) pertaining to the student experience sound appealing?	Beach		
What is one positive feature about this college? One negative feature?	pretty far big	too close to home good school	well known very big
Are my admission chances high, medium or low?	medium	high	low
What is the cost?	$13202	39048	12686
Use this space for notes about this college. Is there anything else you would like to know about the school?			
Grade the school, A to F, on the basis of a good match for you.			

Worksheet 8—College Fact Finder

COLLEGE NAME	UCSC	Uoregon	Claremont mckenna
City & State Distance from a major city? How will I get there?	santa cruz	eugene OR	Claremont
Number of students enrolled?	15688	19528	1261
Does the college offer the academic programs (majors) I'm seeking? If undecided, what programs does the college offer that I'm interested in?			
Life outside of class—Does it seem like an interesting place to be? What features (activities, traditions, location) pertaining to the student experience sound appealing?	outdoorsy	outdoorsy football games	
What is one positive feature about this college? One negative feature?	SC too close big	pretty. too big. too far	5 different schools very small
Are my admission chances high, medium or low?	high	high	low
What is the cost?	13410	27653	42240
Use this space for notes about this college. Is there anything else you would like to know about the school?			
Grade the school, A to F, on the basis of a good match for you.			

mentioned above. There are even guidebooks that have a specific focus. For example, the *ISI Guide to Choosing the Right College* has a more conservative slant.

Get Information Directly From the Colleges

Find opportunities to talk to college representatives. College admission representatives visit high schools or have programs in various cities designed to answer questions of prospective students. Some examples of questions you may want to ask to further your research are: What are the college's strongest departments? What role do fraternities/sororities play in the social life of the college? What financial aid options exist? Any issue important to you should be explored. (Don't let titles of the admission representatives scare you off—colleges have lots of fancy-sounding titles!)

You can also review printed or online material from the colleges. Colleges place lots of material on their websites and they distribute information in their viewbooks and catalogues. If you would like some specific information about features like the women's volleyball team, scholarships based on academic merit, or the program in pre-medicine, ask for it. Read through the material carefully. Keep in mind that colleges put their best foot forward and, thus, these materials may be self-serving. Nonetheless, your systematic review of this information can be productive. Some questions to ask yourself as you read are: What does each college emphasize about itself? What feeling do I get from reading the material or looking at the website? Does the college seem friendly, impersonal, spirited, stuffy, full of rules and requirements, diverse?

Talk to Students

You can talk to students who attend a college of interest, graduates of the college, or those you meet on a campus tour. Recent graduates can tell you a great deal about their collegiate experiences. Ask questions about their major, the effect of the school's location on the campus life, the social opportunities, and so forth. Ask, "What do students like most about your college?" You can often get the names of recent alumni by asking your counselor or by calling the college's admission office. Similarly, you can chat with currently enrolled students. Current students can be helpful as long as they remain objective and as long as they know you. You should ask about their experiences, both in class and in terms of extracurricular activities. You should also plan to talk to students (and not just the tour guide) when you visit campuses.

Access College Websites

You can access college websites through sites such as google.com/options/universities.html, and uscollegesearch.org.

There are websites that allow you to compare colleges on the basis of such criteria as college endowments and graduation rates. For example:

- National Center for Education Statistics, nces.ed.gov/ipedspas/Expt (allows you to compare different colleges)
- General Rankings, library.uiuc.edu/edx/rankings.htm (links to ranking lists like College Prowler list, top colleges for African-Americans, etc.)
- Graduation Rates, collegeresults.org and graduationwatch.com
- Endowments, nacubo.org/x2376.xml
- Public College Values, kiplinger.com/personalfinance/tools/colleges (list of lower cost public colleges)
- US News rankings, usnews.com/usnews/edu/college/rankings/rankindex_brief.php
- National Survey of Student Engagement, nsse.iub.edu
- University & College Accountability Network, ucan-network.org (allows comparisons by tuition, graduation rates, etc.)

You will see a section on Worksheet 8 that asks you to comment on "Life outside of class." Indeed, a key goal of researching is to find out what colleges are like. For example, what students are like, the level of academic pressure, the general nature of social life, and so forth. Knowing about student life on campus (including sports, campus issues, residence hall living, balance of study and socializing) is, in many ways, the most important research dimension, yet finding this information can be difficult. In fact, there are no scientific ways to accurately measure student or academic life. But we can try using the methods described here.

Look at the "student life" section of the college's website to see the clubs offered, the status of fraternities and sororities, the intramural sports opportunities, and so on. Also, websites for particular college cities (the Chamber of Commerce site, for example) can tell you things about the community in which the college is located. This is particularly helpful for smaller, more isolated cities. Is there a symphony orchestra? Are touring Broadway shows common? Are there festivals or activities indigenous to the city? These can be helpful clues to student life. There are also websites that give you some glimpses of campus life. Some of these student life sites are a bit "off the wall." As a result, take details of the review sites with a grain of salt and bear in mind that anyone with a computer can comment on campus life. Here are some of them:

- collegenews.com, access to college newspapers
- collegeprowler.com, descriptions of colleges and reviews
- collegestudentathletes.com, information on athletics
- ed.gov/about/inits/list/whhbcu/edlite-list.html, list of historically black colleges and universities
- epinions.com, search colleges and universities for student reviews
- greekpages.com, information on fraternity and sorority life
- greekspot.com/collegenews, access to college newspapers
- ncaa.com, information on athletics
- newslink.org/statcamp.html, access to college newspapers
- professorprerformance.com, rating of professors (even if you don't know the names of specific faculty members, by reading a few random comments, you can begin to get an idea of teacher/student interaction at a particular school.)
- ratemyprofessors.com, rating of professors
- studentsreview.com, student reviews of colleges
- unigo.com, student reviews of colleges, videos, photos, etc.

Students can also call and/or e-mail various persons on college campuses. You might consider calling a college and talking to a student or asking the admission office for the e-mail address of a student. Or, you can contact a residence hall or the student government or newspaper office. You could find the name of the president of a religious (or other interest) group. Ask the student questions about the college. You might start with, "I'm a high school student and I'm thinking about attending your school. I thought I'd learn about the college by talking to a few students."

Obtain Financial Aid Information

For financial aid and general money issues, students and parents might review *Don't Miss Out: The Ambitious Student's Guide to Financial Aid*. In addition, websites such as those that follow may be helpful:

- act.org/fane, estimate whether you will qualify for need based aid
- collegeanswer.com, Sallie Mae site, a provider of student loans
- collegeboard.com, look at financial aid and cost information
- fafsa.ed.gov, complete the Free Application for Federal Financial Aid
- fastaid.com

- fastweb.monster.com, includes a scholarship search
- federalstudentaid.ed.gov, information on federal student aid
- finaid.org, comprehensive financial aid information source
- freschinfo.com, includes a scholarship search
- money.cnn.com/pf/college, information on the annual cost of tuition
- nasfaa.org
- savingforcollege.com, information on 529 plans
- scholarships.com, includes a scholarship search
- studentaid.org

Review Other Resources

There are books covering topics such as visiting college campuses and essay writing. There are also books intended for students who want guidance on colleges from an ethnic/multicultural perspective. See the Resources for College Planning for a listing of titles.

There are still other sources of information. College videotapes and virtual tours online are made to interest students in a particular college and highlight the positive attributes of the school. One website featuring college videos is campustours.com. For a more unbiased perspective, there are companies that make videos and DVDs of colleges independently. One video option is Collegiate Choice Videos (collegiatechoice.com), and a company that sells DVDs can be found at theu.com. Blogs and photo galleries may also be available through individual college websites.

Filtering Information

Comparing colleges requires you to be a good researcher. Don't rely on one single person for information. Molly Jones, from across the street, may not have had a good experience at College A. Does this mean College A is not right for you? No! It means College A was not right for Molly, who might have been looking for a different type of college than you are. So ask a lot of people and get many perspectives on colleges you are considering. But remember, everyone seems to have an opinion about colleges—friends, parents, relatives, neighbors, and perhaps, even your mail carrier!

Part of your research goal is to separate valid information from information that is old (colleges do change over time), untrue, distorted, prejudiced, or otherwise misguided. Similarly, don't rely on one single book for all of your information on a particular college. Several options are mentioned in this Chapter because multiple sources of information are better than just one. Therefore, ask a lot of people, read a lot, and stay open to new information. The best advice here is to filter all the information and interpret it in a personal manner.

No college is good or bad in the abstract. College A may have the perfect educational program, be the perfect size, be affordable, BUT its location is less than ideal for you. So, what do you do? You're not looking for the perfect college (remember, it probably doesn't exist). Rather, you're looking for a list of several colleges where you will be successful. You should weigh the good points against the bad points and then, ultimately, decide whether that college belongs on your final college list.

Don't let stereotypes guide your choice of colleges. Small colleges are just as much fun as big colleges. More expensive colleges are not inherently "better." More "selective" colleges don't always provide a "better" education. Students in Maine get through winter without dog sleds (or even snowshoes). A degree from a "prestigious" college is not a prerequisite (nor a guarantee) for landing a high-paying job or getting into an excellent graduate school. And the list goes on. The important consideration remains, "Where will I fit in and be successful?"

Don't get frustrated by the volume of material available about each college. Make notes as you go. Don't just say, "all colleges sound the same." Look for differences.

Your impressions are the most important here. You are not looking for "good colleges." Rather, you are looking for good colleges for you. Keep in mind that even among your list of colleges (Worksheet 7), there may be features that do not appeal to you.

No doubt, through your research, you will learn some things about specific colleges that will cause you to stop considering them. For instance, at one school, you might find that fraternities and sororities play a much more significant role in the social scene than you realized or desired, and thus, cross that school off your list.

After you have completed Worksheet 8 (College Fact Finder) for each of your colleges, go back and analyze your research. Sort through your Fact Finders. Look at the notes you made for each school. Besides the overall grade given, look at high and low points for each college. From this analysis, you will have some colleges you like a lot and some that don't quite measure up.

Through this process of elimination, you will be able to refine and reduce your initial list of colleges and move to Worksheet 9 (Your Apply List). Congratulations. This is a great step forward.

Worksheet 9 has spaces for ten colleges, but the number of colleges you apply to will depend on a number of factors. Students apply to more colleges today than a few years ago, but more than eight to ten may mean that you have not done your research.

This is a good time to discuss your list with your counselor and your parents. This list reflects your best thinking about those colleges that seem, on the basis of your research and the "feel" you get, to be places where you would be happy and successful.

Guidelines for Determining Your Likelihood of Admission

As a part of your review of college options, you want to consider your chances of admission. For this task, we could divide colleges into two, three, or even more groupings. We have chosen to look at admission selectivity by dividing your apply list into three categories. Specifically:

1. Low-chance-of-admission colleges are those where your chance of admission is not likely, but still possible. Low-chance-of-admission colleges are sometimes called "reaches."

2. Medium-chance-of-admission colleges are those where your chance of admission is about 50/50. In other words, your chances seem just as good to be admitted as they are to be denied. You also put colleges in this category if you can't place them in either of the other two categories.

3. High-chance-of-admission colleges are those where you will likely be admitted. High-chance-of-admission colleges are often called "safeties" or "backups."

It is very important to keep in mind that no foolproof method exists for separating colleges into these three groups, but the following information may be useful. Be sure to talk with your counselor for help with this task. Ultimately, the goal is not precision, but rather, good judgment.

Here are some guidelines to help determine what categories colleges fall into for you:

1. Carefully consider your admission credentials. Think about the strength of your courses, GPA, test scores, extracurricular activities, and academic curiosity. Think about how you compare to others in your school on these factors. Be realistic. Ask teachers and counselors for input. Look at how you completed Worksheet 4.

2. Compare your GPA and test scores with those listed in the guidebooks for each of your colleges. But remember that high schools vary in their competitiveness—and colleges take the overall quality of your high school into account.

3. Look at the percentage of students admitted. This statistic can be found in guidebooks such as *College Handbook* (you divide those admitted by those who applied) or *Fiske Guide to Colleges*. While the following can vary on the basis of your GPA, test scores, etc., here are some guidelines (not all percentage possibilities are listed below, so use your judgment in differentiating colleges into these categories):

- 30% or lower admission rate colleges may, depending on other factors described here, belong in the low-chance-of-admission category.

- 40–60% admission rate colleges may, depending on other factors described here, belong in the medium-chance-of-admission category.

- Colleges with over 80% of students admitted may, depending on other factors described here, belong in the high-chance-of-admission category.

4. Some guidebooks (*Peterson's*, for example) list colleges on the basis of "Most difficult," "Moderately difficult," etc. Be sure your college list contains colleges from several of these lists.

There are other methods of evaluating your college choices on the basis of admission odds. You should review information from the college itself. This is possible, for example, by asking representatives who visit your high school or by looking at a "profile" of application statistics some colleges make available on their website. Also of interest is the "history" of student acceptances from your high school. Ask your counselor for information on grade point averages or test scores for students who applied from your school to colleges that interest you.

As you do your evaluating, be optimistic as well as realistic. Your "odds" of admission are based on your background, as well as the extent of the competition for places in the freshman class. While comparing yourself with data mined from guidebooks is a first step, you will learn in Chapter 6 that admission officers take many factors into account to determine your "acceptability." Lower test scores, for example, can be offset by strong, college preparatory courses. In addition, your grade point average, extracurricular involvements, level of curiosity, and so forth may suggest a greater or lesser chance of admission. Further, be sure to talk to your college advisor about admission issues and questions. He or she will use knowledge based on experience with many other students to help you make these judgments.

Final Considerations

Here is one additional checklist of questions to consider as you review Worksheet 9 and finalize your apply list:

1. Are colleges included on your list because they fit on the basis of your reading and your general analysis? Your colleges should be more than just "names." Keep in mind that college planning is not just about getting into a top school—it is, more importantly, about fitting in and being happy.

2. Does your list of schools represent a good match of your interests and talents, as well as the strengths of the colleges?

3. Do you have some appealing high-chance-of-admission ("backup") colleges? Having solid backups is important, especially in these days of increased college selectivity. Some students spend a great deal of time deciding on their low chance ("reach") colleges and relatively little time choosing their backups. Your backups are important to good college planning. A balance is what you are looking for in terms of admission selectivity. Let's assume you apply to eight colleges. In that case, you will want one or two schools from your "low-chance-of-admission" list, two or three from your "medium-chance" list, and two or three from your "high-chance" list.

4. Do you have a financial safety school? This is the college (perhaps a local state university) where cost is agreeable with your parents.

If the answer to any of these questions is "no," you should rethink your college selection criteria and talk with your advisors. If the answers are "yes," congratulations! You are on the road to a good college choice.

Use this data to determine whether you need to expand or shrink your apply list.

Worksheet 9—Your Apply List

College Name	Location
1.	
2.	
3.	
4.	
5.	
6.	
7.	
8.	
9.	
10.	

Application Completion: Keeping on Track

Next, complete Worksheet 10 (Application Timetable). This timetable will help you get organized and monitor the numerous deadlines associated with applying to college. You should complete Worksheet 10 as follows:

Step One. Complete the left column with the name of each college you will apply to. This list comes from Worksheet 9. If you apply to more than eight colleges, make a copy of the timetable. Read the application materials for each college thoroughly. Be aware of procedures applicable to each of your college choices. In addition, find out how your school processes applications. What are your responsibilities? Is your high school responsible for mailing your transcript and/or your application? If you apply online, how will your transcript and teacher recommendations be sent? Are completed teacher recommendations given to you, sent directly to the college, or given to the counseling office?

Step Two. Fill in the column labeled, "Admission Chances." You are determining, to the best of your ability, the level of selectivity for each of your college choices. Is the college a low chance of admission school (a "reach"), a high chance of admission school (a "backup"), or a medium chance of admission school? (Look at the box, "Guidelines for

Determining your Likelihood of Admission" on page 89 for guidance on this process.) Make sure you have at least one college in each category.

Step Three. Check to see how you will apply to the college—that is the "Application Method." Does the college use a paper or online application? Many schools let you apply electronically from their own website. Over 350 colleges accept the "Common Application" (commonapp.org) and over 80 accept the Universal Application (universalcollegeapp.com). If you are using the Common Application also check to see if the college requests any supplementary material. Do you have an application or know how to access one? If you do not, go to the perspective student/admission section of the college website and complete an information request form, e-mail or call to receive an application.

Step Four. Record the deadline for submission of the application for each college.

Step Five. After you know when the application is due, establish your own target date for submitting your application. This will keep you organized and moving forward during the fall of your Senior year. Look at the application deadlines; your target date should be well in advance to the deadline set by the college in order to give yourself time to complete the application and the essays in an unhurried way. Many students try to complete all of their applications by Thanksgiving of their Senior year; others try to have them in the mail by winter vacation.

Step Six. In the next column, record each of your essay topics. Most colleges ask students to write an essay. Some require only one, while a few very selective schools require one or two major essays, as well as a number of shorter paragraphs. Be sure to list all writing tasks given to you—essays, personal statements, short answers, and brief paragraphs. With this list, you can tell which assignments are most common and whether there are any overlapping topics (in other words, essays you can adapt for more than one college). From here, you can systematically begin writing. Start work on your essays well before the application due date to give yourself time to refine and polish your writing. You'll find essay strategies in Chapter 6.

Step Seven. The next two columns deal with recommendations. A recommendation from your high school counselor is commonly required. In addition, many colleges ask for teacher recommendations. For each of your colleges, check to see what recommendations are necessary. Do you need to meet with your counselor in order for him/her to prepare a recommendation for you? Have you asked your teachers? How are the recommendations transmitted to the college?

Worksheet 10 — Application Timetable

College or University	Admission Chances	Application Method	Application Deadline	My Target Date for Submitting Application
1.				
2.				
3.				
4.				
5.				
6.				
7.				
8.				

Worksheet 10 — Application Timetable (cont'd)

Topic of Essay(s)	Date Recommendations Requested/Sent	Date Test Scores Requested/ Sent	Other (What?)	Other (What?)	Other (What?)

Step Eight. In the next column, record what tests the colleges require for admission and indicate the date you have your scores sent. Usually, you notify the testing agency (College Board or ACT) to send your scores directly to your colleges.

Step Nine. The remaining columns (labeled "Other: What?) allow you to personalize the Application Timetable. What other documents are needed? You may, for example, use one of the columns to track required financial aid forms (and deadlines), and a second column to indicate the date of your music audition or your contacts with a coach. This may also be the place to record the deadline for applying for on-campus housing. Record how you are going to use the columns in the blank spaces at the top of the Timetable.

Keeping track of all this information allows you to stay focused during a busy time in your life. Taking just a few minutes each week to see where you are, allowing time to complete essays, etc., will make a big difference in your sanity during your Senior year.

Now that you have identified and compared colleges, the next Chapter focuses on an important way to learn about a college: the campus visit.

CHAPTER 5

∎∎∎∎∎∎∎∎∎∎∎∎∎∎∎∎∎∎∎∎

LEARNING FROM CAMPUS VISITS

The process of making a good college choice involves several important steps. By considering your goals, your interests, and your achievements, you have begun the process of considering colleges and comparing them to your requirements and ideals.

Common Questions About Campus Visits

Chapter 4 presented the variety of resources available to help you make a good college choice. Your parents, college advisors, and a variety of publications will give you some sense of the life at a particular college. But *one* important way for you to know if you might feel comfortable is to visit the college itself and observe your own reactions to the campus, the people, and the general atmosphere of the college. This chapter answers the questions most commonly asked about campus visits.

1. Why should I visit colleges?

The best reason for visiting is to learn about the college first-hand. Usually students return from college visits with new impressions and perspectives about places they previously knew only from websites, written material or the comments of others. Campus visits bring colleges to life, and they're an excellent way for you to find out if the college will be a good place for you to live for four years. So visit to learn more—to help with the fact-finding process. While few colleges still require on-campus interviews, and seldom will such meetings be the critical factor in a decision on your application, visits do show your interest in the school. In sum, visitation can be very helpful in your college shopping.

If cost or time are issues, use other resources to find out about your potential college choices—at least in the initial phases of your investigation. Remember the sources of college information mentioned in the last chapter.

2. How should I prepare for campus visits?

Although it sounds obvious, you must first decide which colleges you will visit. While you may have neither time nor resources to visit all the colleges your counselor recommends, neither should you visit only those that are the most competitive for you. In general, you should plan campus visits to four or five schools that represent different levels of competitiveness and choice for you. Chapter 4 discussed ways to think about your chances of admission. Ideally, you should visit your first or second choice schools only after visiting others. You will profit from the experience and the perspective you gain.

3. When should I visit colleges?

The best time to visit colleges will vary for each student. If you have planned well ahead and have identified colleges appropriate for you, the spring of your junior year is a good time to see campuses. Very long-term planners might visit in the spring of the sophomore year.

Many students visit campuses during the summer between their junior and senior years. While this is not the best time to see a campus "in action" (since those students on campus may not be representative of those who attend between September and June), it's a relaxed time for admission staffs—and, perhaps, the easiest time for families to get away. Often, entire families tour colleges together, combining visits with vacations. If you're not careful, summer visits can become "architectural tours." While the beauty of the buildings and campus greenery are important, students and teachers contribute most to a good college experience. Campus beauty— and weather conditions—are secondary to your fit with the other students.

The fall or winter of your senior year is a good time to see the campus, and at some schools, the best time to meet someone from the admission office. Some selective colleges fill their appointment schedule early, so, the key words for visits to highly selective college campuses are: call early.

The spring of your senior year, after you have received all your admission decisions, is a good time to visit and make your final choice. Unfortunately, admission offices can be quite hectic at this time of year and making travel arrangements without much advanced planning can be expensive.

If you participate in a sport, and you want to continue that sport while in college, you may want to visit campuses while your sport is "in season."

Your other decision is what day of the week to visit. To gain a real sense of campus life—meet some students, sit in on classes and participate in some typical activities—then you should schedule your visits during weekdays of the regular school year. While some admission offices are open on Saturday mornings, most campuses are fairly quiet on weekends. Also, to get a good sense of a campus and its people, you want to visit on a "normal" day, so avoid exam weeks and big football game weekends.

Whatever your schedule is like, remember that campus visits will be most beneficial if they occur after you have discussed college options with your counselor and completed your own research on recommended colleges (and completed Worksheet 8 in Chapter 4). Don't just "head West" (or any other direction, for that matter) to visit colleges in a willy-nilly fashion.

4. I am visiting several colleges in one trip. How much time should I spend on each campus?

Try to spend as much time as possible at each college. An overnight stay is ideal. Most students need at least half a day for each visit; a visit of less than three hours is insufficient for a complete view of a college.

5. What should be done before I visit?

Arrange for your visit by calling or e-mailing the admission office at each school you plan to visit. Call or e-mail several weeks in advance of your desired visit. Be aware that the *most* selective colleges fill up interview times several months ahead, although it is still possible to have a campus tour or an information session. Information sessions are described in Question 10.

If you do not stay on the campus, ask the admission office for recommendations about motels or hotels nearby. Schedule your appointments so you can arrive on time. Study road maps and transportation schedules; allow extra time to find a college if you are unfamiliar with the region or city in which it is located.

There is often a set routine that involves a campus tour and may include a meeting with someone from the admission office or a general information session (see #10). Note: As you will read in #8 below, "meetings" with admission officers at colleges these days are seldom "interviews" in the formal sense; rather they are often non-evaluative discussions or talks.

Sometimes you can tell the admission office what you would like to do during your visit—take a tour, meet with a member of the admission staff, attend a class, meet with a professor and eat in a dining hall—and they will arrange it. Othertimes you will be asked to make calls to other offices to arrange features of your visit. Some students meet with a coach, others want to see the studio art facilities. Your visit depends on your interests.

If possible, spend a night in a campus residence hall. If you know students on the campus, call them and ask if you can be their guest for a night or if they have time to spend with you when you visit.

Whatever you do, talk to as many students as you can during your visit. Also pay attention to bulletin boards and the campus newspaper; both are good guides to campus activities. See the list of "dos and don'ts" later in this chapter.

6. What sort of questions should I ask?

Since the purpose of your college visits is to research your level of comfort at the schools, plan your questions accordingly. Some questions may be general and apply to every school you visit; others may be more specific. You will gain the most insight into the school you visit if your questions go beyond the obvious—the ones answered in the factual publications or on college web sites. Ask questions about those issues and topics that matter to you. Don't hesitate to ask the nitty-gritty questions.

To arrive at questions important *to you*, review the characteristics of your ideal college, Worksheet 6. A few general questions follow.

Questions to ask students or admission officers:

- Why do students select this college?
- What do students on campus rave about?
- What do students complain about most?
- Describe the sort of students who thrive here and the kinds of students who are most unhappy here.
- How active is the social life?
- What type of student seems happiest here?
- What are the most popular majors?
- What are the most popular extracurricular activities?
- What are the opportunities for extracurricular participation?
- What are student traditions?
- How active is the college in helping students with career planning?
- What happens here on weekends? Do students stay on campus?
- How safe is your campus? How comfortable will I feel walking through your campus alone at night?
- Do students know one or two professors well enough to ask them for a work or a graduate school recommendation? What help will I get?

- How good is the faculty advising for selecting classes and fulfilling requirements?
- (For students) When did you last meet individually with a professor?
- How are roommates chosen?
- How much time do students spend on homework each week?
- How often are things learned *in* class discussed *outside* class?
- What do faculty members expect of students?
- How "electronic" is the campus? Are syllabi or other resources available online? Can papers be submitted electronically?
- How would you evaluate the balance between spending time on academics and spending time on personal and social things?

Questions to ask admission officers or professors:
- What are typical course requirements—how many exams, papers, etc.?
- Who teaches introductory courses—professors or graduate students?
- What arrangements are made for advising and tutorial help?
- What opportunities exist for independent study and study abroad?
- What departments are considered outstanding, weak, and average?
- After graduation, what do students do? Go to grad school? Get a job?
- What constitutes a typical freshman-year program?
- Why is this a good college for me to study my selected major?
- What if I am unsure about my major? What kind of feedback do students get on coursework and how often do they get it? Is this a good place to explore?
- What types of tutoring opportunities are available?
- Do most students study abroad?
- Are internships or independent study opportunities common?

Having asked these questions and others, your campus visits will be most beneficial if you use Worksheet 11 to make notes after each visit.

7. Should my parents go with me?

Parents can be great for helping you determine your level of comfort and your ability to succeed at a given college. Also, parents often have questions of their own. They do have an investment—financial and otherwise—in your plans for the future. While parents can be helpful and supportive throughout the visit, they should not participate in the personal meeting with admission officers. Perhaps they will want to schedule a visit with a financial aid officer or just walk around the campus while you are involved in an admission meeting. Following your visit, share your reactions and observations with your parents before asking for their impressions. Then weigh their comments with yours as you think about each college.

8. What is a personal interview on campus and how important is it?

An interview is most often a general discussion with the student about past educational attainment, interests and motivation toward college. Further, the personal interview is rarely a required part of the admission process, and is seldom a deciding factor in accepting or rejecting a candidate. An interview does not transform an unacceptable applicant into an acceptable one. An interview can, however, be an excellent way to learn about a college. It is a two-way exchange. You should be ready to ask questions that will help you learn more about the college, and be ready to answer questions that will help the interviewer learn more about you. Some typical questions and requests follow:

- Tell me something about yourself as a student.
- How did you become interested in this college?
- What things are most important to you as you compare colleges?
- What are your interests, strengths, and weaknesses?
- Do you have any questions? (This is usually asked. Be ready!)

Do not hesitate to identify one or two things about yourself you want the interviewer to know as the result of talking with you, and be sure to mention them when the interviewer says, "Is there anything else we should know about you?"

In addition, do not hesitate to share the leadership of the conversation. You are not on the witness stand; it is not a "grilling." You should use your time with an admission officer as a chance to see if the college fits you, too. Moreover, colleges will want to make both your campus visit and your interview a positive experience for you.

Also, many selective colleges will grant local interviews with alums; these are helpful and alumni/ae can be valuable sources of information about a college. Remember, however, alums are likely to be volunteers, not employees of the university. As such, their level of current information about the college varies considerably.

9. What should I do if I meet with an admission representative?

Here are a few tips:

- Dress comfortably. Wear regular school clothing.
- Be honest and be yourself. Do not try to second guess what the interviewer wants to hear.
- Ask questions.
- Make eye contact.
- Make a note of the person's name.
- Try to find out where you stand. Near the end of the meeting, ask about your admission chances based on the information you've shared.

10. What are information sessions?

If you don't desire a personal meeting or if the college doesn't offer them, ask if the school provides a group information session. At these meetings, an admission officer speaks to a group of prospective students and parents, and then often addresses their individual questions.

11. Do colleges ever have special days when prospective students can visit?

Yes, many colleges schedule special visitation days for prospective students. During a college-day program, a school often focuses all its resources on the needs of visitors. If you enjoy other students and like to participate as a member of a group of students, the college visit program will be an exciting experience. If you want more individual attention, you should schedule an individual visit.

12. What should I do after the visit?

Mail (or e-mail) a thank-you note to those who were helpful on your visit. This is a gracious and polite response to those who assisted you. If you met with an admission officer, mention something about the meeting that impressed you, and that will enable the interviewer to remember you.

13. What other resources can I use?

Professor Pathfinder's US College and University Reference Map (hedbergmaps.com) is a useful tool for learning about locations of colleges and for planning travel to college campus. In addition, *The College Atlas and Planner* (wintergreenorchardhouse.com) is helpful.

14. My family's funds are limited. We can't afford a tour of colleges. How can I learn about colleges?

In most cases, you need not travel thousands of miles to learn about colleges, just visit a few colleges in your state. Choose nearby schools;

private, small liberal arts colleges as well as medium or large state universities. These visits will help you get the feel of different types of institutions—you can visit the schools to which you have been admitted later. Attend any campus visit programs sponsored by colleges near you. Sit in on a class and, most importantly, talk to students. Talk to currently enrolled college students when they are home on vacation. Attend college night programs at your high school. Visit with college alumni. Or, finally, telephone or e-mail the admission office and request that a student be in touch with you to talk about the college. Most importantly, look at Chapter 4 for other ways to explore college options.

15. How can I tell if a college is a good one for me?

View the visit as one important way to assess a college, not as the only way. Keep in mind what you have learned in this book about the characteristics of your ideal college. Measure what you see and hear against the qualities you listed as important on Worksheet 6 in Chapter 3. But a few final tips are in order:

- *Do* record your observations. Use Worksheet 11.
- *Do* talk to students on every campus.
- *Do* follow up your visit with a thank-you note.
- *Do Not* evaluate the school on the basis of a visit with one student.
- *Do Not* judge a college solely on your impressions of the tour guide.
- *Do* analyze the whole school.
- *Do* take photographs.
- *Do* read copies of the student newspaper.
- *Do* look at the bulletin boards and other postings. What's happening on campus? Do these activities interest you?
- *Do* roam the campus by yourself—look for clues that the college is a place where you would fit in.
- *Do* walk or drive around the community surrounding the college.
- *Do* go to the student activities office. What clubs are most popular? Are first-year students able to get involved in most organizations? Does one type of activity—sports, Greek letter organizations, the local bar scene—seem to dominate?
- *Do* check out the public transportation system.
- *Do* try to determine: Does the school seem like an interesting place for ME to be?

- *Do Not* let the weather on the day of your visit totally influence your impression.
- *Do Not* make snap judgments.
- *Do* judge schools after you return home and have time to think about all of your visits.
- *Do Not* let perceived quality or academic reputation totally affect you. Your task is to find the right colleges for *you*.
- *Do Not* judge the college *solely* on impressions made on your visit. Remember what you have read and heard about the college before your visit.

16. How can I remember my impressions of each college?

Write them down! *Campus Visit Notes* are provided for four colleges using Worksheet 11. Make a copy of the worksheet for each additional campus you visit.

Write notes @ visits

Worksheet 11—Campus Visit Notes

Name of College _____

Location _____

Date of Visit _____

Names of people you spoke to:

_____

_____

Campus Facilities:

Comments on how the campus strikes you.

_____

_____

_____

_____

_____

Student Life:

Comments about student life on campus. Is there a good chance I could fit in with the students?

_____

_____

_____

_____

_____

Academic Factors:

Comments about academics. Does this seem like the right place for me to study and learn?

_____

_____

_____

_____

_____

Overall Impressions:
What did you like best?

_____

_____

_____

_____

_____

What did you like least?

_____

_____

_____

_____

_____

Other Facts You Want To Remember About This College:

_____

_____

_____

_____

_____

Overall Assessment Of How Well This College Fits You:

Not Very Well   1   2   3   4   5   Extremely Well

Worksheet 11—Campus Visit Notes

Name of College _____

    Location   _____

    Date of Visit _____

    Names of people you spoke to:

_____

_____

Campus Facilities:

Comments on how the campus strikes you.

_____

_____

_____

_____

_____

Student Life:

Comments about student life on campus. Is there a good chance I could fit in with the students?

_____

_____

_____

_____

_____

Academic Factors:

Comments about academics. Does this seem like the right place for me to study and learn?

_____

_____

_____

_____

_____

Overall Impressions:
What did you like best?

_____

_____

_____

_____

What did you like least?

_____

_____

_____

_____

Other Facts You Want To Remember About This College:

_____

_____

_____

_____

Overall Assessment Of How Well This College Fits You:

Not Very Well   1   2   3   4   5   Extremely Well

Worksheet 11—Campus Visit Notes

Name of College _____

Location _____

Date of Visit _____

Names of people you spoke to:

_____

_____

Campus Facilities:

Comments on how the campus strikes you.

_____

_____

_____

_____

_____

Student Life:

Comments about student life on campus. Is there a good chance I could fit in with the students?

_____

_____

_____

_____

_____

Academic Factors:

Comments about academics. Does this seem like the right place for me to study and learn?

_____

_____

_____

_____

_____

Overall Impressions:
  What did you like best?

_____

_____

_____

_____

  What did you like least?

_____

_____

_____

_____

Other Facts You Want To Remember About This College:

_____

_____

_____

_____

Overall Assessment Of How Well This College Fits You:

Not Very Well   1   2   3   4   5   Extremely Well

Worksheet 11—Campus Visit Notes

Name of College _____

    Location _____

    Date of Visit _____

    Names of people you spoke to:

_____

_____

Campus Facilities:

    Comments on how the campus strikes you.

_____

_____

_____

_____

_____

Student Life:

    Comments about student life on campus. Is there a good chance I could fit in with the students?

_____

_____

_____

_____

_____

Academic Factors:

    Comments about academics. Does this seem like the right place for me to study and learn?

_____

_____

_____

_____

_____

Overall Impressions:
   What did you like best?

_____

_____

_____

_____

_____

   What did you like least?

_____

_____

_____

_____

_____

Other Facts You Want To Remember About This College:

_____

_____

_____

_____

_____

Overall Assessment Of How Well This College Fits You:

Not Very Well   1   2   3   4   5   Extremely Well

CHAPTER 6

■■■■■■■■■■■■■■■■■■■

MAKING YOUR ESSAYS WORK FOR YOU

You have, at this point, already made some important decisions about the colleges you will consider as well as the colleges to which you will apply. Now, you are ready to begin the process of preparing your college essay. The essay, more accurately called a "personal statement" since it varies from a traditional essay written for a school assignment, is usually the most time-consuming part of the application, and it deserves the most attention.

This chapter is divided into three sections. First, you will complete Worksheet 12 which explains the reasoning behind the essay questions commonly found on applications and assists you in thinking through your answers. Second, you will complete Worksheet 13 which presents opportunities to brainstorm additional essay ideas. And third, you'll get some specific hints for writing excellent and highly communicative essays.

This chapter, however, does *not* include complete essays used by students for their own college applications because such samples may impair your own creativity and constrain your thinking. No essays are generically "good" or "bad" or "right" or "wrong." There are only good or bad essays *for you.* Everyone has his/her own special qualities and stories to tell. And those stories are the substance of good essays.

Before You Start

First, in case you are wondering, colleges do read your essays. While a few large universities rely primarily on grade point averages and test scores to make admission decisions, the vast majority of admission committees actually read, study, and think carefully about the words you write on your essays. In fact, at some colleges, your application will be read by two, three, or more people. Moreover, your application may be discussed at length by a group of admission people in a committee meeting. The application essay, then, should communicate, on paper, what you would like a group of strangers to know about you. Many students are unused to using words and paper as a key way of communicating images of themselves, and this makes applications and essays difficult for many students.

Perhaps the most formidable barrier to essay writing is a lack of confidence about writing in general and personal writing in specific. Many students start the process by wondering what colleges want to see in an essay. This type of thinking is a waste of time! Don't try to "psyche out" an admission committee by deciding what it wants to read. Rather, the most important question you can ask yourself is: What is it about me that I want colleges to know? Colleges are vitally interested in knowing about you, your interests, your feelings, your reactions, your insights, your qualities, your passions, your satisfactions and your disappointments, to name but a few. The extent to which you tell your own meaningful story in an interesting, readable and articulate way is the extent to which your essay is good.

No easy, quick solution is offered here for building writing confidence. But, often, students are surprised to find that the incident or reaction they thought most unsuitable for a college essay is exactly the one that is most important and revealing about them. Do not try to be anyone else in your essay. Tell about yourself and you'll write a wonderful essay! (Note: Sometimes your parents think you are so terrific they want you to tell the colleges how terrific you are. While their intent is admirable, your essay should not seem as if you are patting yourself on the back—save that for someone else!)

In their applications, colleges ask a variety of essay questions. Some questions are specific ("Tell us how a book you read in the last year has influenced you") and others are very broad and general ("Tell us something about yourself that will help us get to know you better").

Many colleges call the essay a personal statement, some make the essay optional, and some require no essay at all. With few exceptions, though, most students gain by enclosing a personal statement with their application (even when it is not required). Worksheet 12 lists common essay questions with a series of brainstorming strategies for each. In fact, many of the essay topics in this chapter are from two commonly used generic applications: The Common Application (commonapp.org) and the Universal Application (universalapp.com). By brainstorming, you'll arrive at one or two ideas you can use in preparing your own (yes, your very own) answer to the question.

After you complete Worksheet 12, move right on to Worksheet 13. Your answers to these open-ended questions may suggest other topics to consider as you begin working on your own applications. These two worksheets should give you a head start on your essay writing.

After you finish this chapter, and after you identify your college choices, make a list of all the essays, personal statements or other writing assignments your colleges require. Then, prioritize your writing requirements on the basis of application deadlines and your own target dates, as listed in Chapter 4, Worksheet 10.

Worksheet 12—Tackling Sample Essay Questions

Topic 1—Evaluate a significant experience, achievement, risk you have taken, or ethical dilemma you have faced and its impact on you.
Of all the questions asked by colleges, this is perhaps the most common. It provides you with an amazing number of opportunities to write about those aspects of your life that are most important to you.

The word "significant" in this question is critical because it requires personal reflection; an experience, or achievement, etc. becomes significant when it causes us to see ourselves or others in a new or different way. In other words, just because you've never weathered a typhoon or won a national ski racing championship doesn't mean you're wanting for "significant" experiences. Even at seventeen, you've had experiences that have affected you deeply; experiences others will find interesting. For example, one student produced a very thoughtful essay about the changes that occurred at home when her mom decided to go to college full-time. Another student wrote about the significance of visiting his grandmother every summer on a farm in Nebraska. Still another student received a traffic ticket and wrote about his reactions to and learnings from his encounter with the law. Another student completed a very interesting description about the expanded family he gained when his mother remarried.

As you reflect on possible topics, remember, an experience that affects you has no prescribed length. An important experience may last several minutes, several hours, days, or months. The most important consideration is that the experience had a memorable impact on you. In this essay, you will describe the experience and how you felt about it and discuss what it reveals about you.

The same considerations apply if you consider a risk you have taken or an ethical dilemma you have faced. In either case, it's important that your essay reveals an element of your personality. The risk or the dilemma is less important than what you learned. Remember that conflicting feelings, change and uncertainty are the "stuff" upon which good essays are made.

Try this: Close your eyes, and for a few minutes go through your memory bank. Think about everything that's happened to you since you became a high school freshman. No doubt a few of those memories are a bit more vivid, a bit more clear than others. Normally, those vivid memories are or were "significant" experiences.

Now you try. Briefly list a few of your significant experiences:

Excellent! Now, in a few phrases, explain why one of those experiences was significant. What did you learn about yourself as the result of the experience? Here's how one student began:

My younger brother's struggle with a severe hearing loss has affected me significantly because I have had to grow up rapidly and assume some added responsibilities at home. Sometimes it's real scary, because I don't exactly know how to do the things I am expected to do in taking care of him.

It's your turn below:

Terrific! You have the beginnings of the essay about a significant experience. If the question directs you to write about a significant achievement or accomplishment, you will do the same kind of thinking.

Topic 2—Briefly elaborate on one of your extracurricular activities or work experiences.

This question is relatively easy. Think about everything you do to occupy your time when you are not in school or studying. Refer to Your Activities/ Experiences Record, Worksheet 3. Do you play the piano, sew your own clothes, play sports or write articles for the school paper? Do you work, take care of a baby brother, or volunteer at a nursing home? The key here is identifying an activity that has meaning for you. First, list the meaningful activity:

_____

_____

_____

Now think about the ways in which the activity has been meaningful for you. As you think, go beyond the obvious. It is normal, for instance, that a team sport like soccer might be meaningful because you learned teamwork. But no doubt you also learned a great deal more than teamwork by playing soccer. Did you learn how to deal with disappointment? Did you learn that "people skills" are not as easy as you thought? This is one student's thesis about her experiences as a field hockey player:

> *Playing field hockey last year was significant for me. I learned that I am not as good a leader as I am a follower, and for the first time, I learned how to deal with people I don't like.*

Now, write a sentence or two that tells, specifically, the way or ways in which the activity you listed above has been meaningful or significant for you.

_____

_____

_____

_____

_____

_____

Great! You've just written the thesis sentence for an essay regarding a meaningful activity. In the Hints Section later in this chapter, you'll find some suggestions on how to develop the sentence above into a complete essay about an important activity.

Topic 3—Discuss your educational and/or your career objectives.

This question stumps many students. Often it is not easy for them to identify or name their plans for the future. But, for just a minute, think about why you want to go to college. Look back at your Self-Survey results (Worksheet 2). What did you learn about yourself as you thought about your answers in such categories as "School Enthusiasm," "Career Orientation" and "Eagerness for College?" Some of your thoughts may become your answer to a question about your educational goals. Again, go beyond the obvious. Many students say they want to go to college to get a job. But think about those things that you want to learn in college that will make you a better employee or employer.

Now list below three reasons why you want to go to college:

a. _to be successful in life_

b. _to obtain knowledge past high school_

c. _to be able to have a good career_

Next, think about your personal and professional goals. Do not feel awkward if you have no idea what you want to do when you get older. You may simply want to list the careers you have considered and provide a brief statement explaining why or how you have thought about each field. Maybe friends or family have suggested various career ideas to you and you may have thought seriously about a few of those. Or, ask yourself: If I were paid an excellent salary to do what I like best, regardless of stature or social value, what would I do with my life? Such issues and questions are often a good beginning to career exploration.

Using the space below, write an answer to the question: What are your thoughts or ideas about your career or professional goals?

If I go into a field with a masters program, I want to for sure get my masters. I do not really know what I want to do. My family has suggested child psychology because

I work well w/kids; a lawyer b/c I argue logically.

But what if the question also asks you to list your personal goals? Don't worry; simply think about those aspects of your personal life that college might change or expand. For instance, perhaps you're looking forward to meeting new friends, to becoming more independent, to learning about a different part of the country, to joining a service organization, to trying an activity or skill you've never done before. All of those can comprise the personal goals you'd like to accomplish in college.

If an essay topic asks for some personal goals, state a few ideas below:

- Make new friends
- experience/learn to live on my own
- learn about myself
- learn about other parts of the world, maybe study abroad

Topic 4—Why have you selected University of the Universe? Or, what would you bring to the diversity of our college community?

Some colleges may ask why you selected their particular institution as a school to which you will apply. At this point, all your prior good thinking and research will come into good use. Review the factors you listed as important in selecting a college, specifically Worksheet 6 in Chapter 3. Let's say you are applying to the fictitious 'University of the Universe' (UOU). Compare those factors to the distinguishing features of the UOU. You should find that many features at UOU fit the criteria you feel are important in your college choice. For example, UOU may be perfect because you were seeking a small liberal arts college with friendly students located in a rural area. For this essay, list the qualities that led you to choose that particular college. You might also indicate other factors that promoted your interest. Perhaps you visited UOU or talked to its representative. Or you may have been impressed with what alumni said about UOU. All these may be reasons why you feel UOU is a good choice.

As for adding to the diversity of the college community, consider, as you did with other topics, the person you are and the life experiences you've had. One can add to diversity through ideas, cultural/religious/ethnic heritage, interests, perspectives on the world, and so on.

First, list one of your current favorite colleges:

_____

Second, either describe why you would like to attend or what you would bring to the diversity of the campus community:

_____

_____

_____

_____

_____

_____

_____

_____

Topic 5—Indicate a person who has had a significant influence on you and describe that influence.

Again, go through your memory bank to those persons (friends, family, teachers, coaches, clergy, etc.) who have had an impact on you. Think about the ways in which each of these people influenced you or caused you to change? What did this person teach you? What role model or behavioral example did this person set for you? Be specific. Talk about particular instances in which this person displayed for you the influence he/she had. And the most important part of this question: Identify, in precise language, the reasons you selected the person you chose. It is not enough to say, "I admire my Uncle Sam because he is a kind person." You must connect the quality of kindness to you. Do you admire Uncle Sam's kindness because it is a quality you are trying to emulate yourself? Or do you see the kindness he displays as similar to but different from the kind acts you do?

Remember, the point of the essay is to tell the admission committee something about you. You are simply using the impact and qualities of a significant person to tell your story.

First, write the name of a person who has had an influence on your life:

_____

Now, state one thing about that influence:

_____

_____

_____

_____

_____

_____

_____

Topic 6—Tell us something about yourself that might be helpful to our understanding of you. Or, simply, write on a topic of your choice.

Talk about open-ended! The key here is to choose some aspect of yourself, your background, your family, your activities, or your accomplishments on which to focus. *Do not* try to tell the committee everything there is to know about you in 300 words! It can't be done, and if you try, it is likely to be a boring recital of every award, contest or honor you ever won. For this response, choose one significant feature, describe it completely and in a compelling fashion, and tell your reader your own reactions or responses. This is the beginning of one student's response:

> *Something that might not otherwise come through the statistics of this application is that I don't mind getting dirty. Besides being a kid for most of my life, I've worked with a lot of children. From children, I have learned that the point of a puddle is to jump in it, the idea behind clay is to get it under one's fingernails, and walls are constructed to do handstands against.*

This student went on to talk about the effect of "getting dirty" on her life. She related various specific instances of the "messy" process of trial and error as it affected her education and her desire for her college education.

By now, it should be clear that a simple listing of awards and accomplishments does not help your reader learn about you. If your reader is to gain any sense of the person you are, you must write of your reactions and feelings towards those awards, defeats and accomplishments. A list of awards is simply that, a list.

OK, now try yourself. What is one thing would you like a college to know about you?

_____

_____

_____

_____

_____

_____

Topic 7—Describe a significant academic experience. Or, describe a character in fiction, a historical figure, or a creative work that has had an influence on you.

A significant academic experience can be a particular class you liked. Think about why the class was good. Was it the characteristics of the teacher? Was the subject material particularly fascinating? Did you like the assignments? And be specific about the ways that class made you think and grow. A significant academic experience can also be a particular book or project or experiment in which you became totally absorbed. What made the book or project or experiment so exciting to you? Finally, an academic experience can be significant because you really worked hard to understand a topic or a concept and finally mastered it. Here's how one student started:

> *Reading* Winnie the Pooh *again in my junior literature class was significant for me. Winnie, you see, is my hero. He never gets down on himself, never panics in a crisis, and fills his living space with hummed tunes and poetry. I learned that superior literature can be simple. I know that important messages in life come from basic as well as complex words. I appreciate the straightforwardness of* Winnie the Pooh, *but also the depth of analysis that is possible within one's imagination and creativity.*

In the following space, jot down an idea or two about a significant academic experience:

_____

_____

_____

_____

_____

Another way to answer this question is to consider the extent to which you have lived up to your potential as a high school student. Think about yourself as a student. If you have worked up to your potential, write a brief statement about your strengths as a student. For example, were you successful because of your organizational skills? Your willingness to work hard? Your excellent teachers? If you have not yet worked up to your abilities, why not? There may be perfectly valid reasons—illness, learning difficulties or changes of high schools. Or was it a lack of motivation, or did you place a priority on your out-of-school activities? If some real barriers have impeded your success, you should feel comfortable talking about them.

Have you lived up to your potential in high school? Why or why not?

_____

_____

_____

_____

_____

_____

_____

_____

_____

Topic 8—Discuss some issue of personal, local, national, or international concern and its importance to you.

These questions are not as dissimilar as they look. The key to your responses is to link them to yourself, your feelings and your experiences. You may be concerned about the environment, but unless you have a personal connection to the topic of recycling, for example, your essay may be little more than an objective (hence not personal) discussion of that topic. The best topic for the "issue" essay is a topic about which you feel so strongly you could write an editorial for your school or city paper. Your reader is most often uninterested in an expository essay; as with all the other topics, you should use the issue as a means of telling about you, the topic about whom your readers really want to know.

As practice, use the following space to tell about an issue of concern:

_____

_____

_____

_____

_____

_____

_____

Worksheet 13—Essay Brainstorming

The eight questions provided in Worksheet 12 commonly appear on college applications; however, as indicated earlier, the possibilities for essay questions are endless. Don't let the questions stump you; remember, the central purpose of the essay, regardless of the specific question, is to let the admission committee get to know you. So, if your applications contain questions not among the eight just discussed, use the following exercises to give you ideas on ways to answer the uncommon question.

Listed below is a series of adjectives. Quickly circle those words you feel are true about you most of the time.

able	determined	independent	original	respectful
accepting	direct	ingenious	overconfident	responsible
active	diplomatic	innovative	passive	retentive
adaptable	disciplined	inspiring	paternal	scientific
aggressive	doer	intelligent	perceptive	self-reliant
ambitious	driver	introverted	perfectionist	sensible
analytical	efficient	intuitive	persuasive	sensitive
articulate	energetic	jovial	playful	sentimental

assertive	enterprising	kind	pleasant	serious
aware	enthusiastic	knowledgeable	powerful	sincere
brave	extroverted	lazy	practical	skillful
calm	fair	leader	precise	sophisticated
carefree	flexible	liberal	principled	sociable
caring	follower	lively	progressive	spontaneous
cheerful	frank	logical	protective	stable
clever	free	loving	proud	strong
competent	friendly	loyal	punctual	supportive
competitive	genial	maternal	questioning	sympathetic
confident	gentle	mature	quiet	tactful
conforming	giving	merry	radical	thoughtful
conscientious	gregarious	modest	rational	tolerant
cooperative	gullible	methodical	realistic	tough
courageous	happy	naive	reasonable	trustworthy
creative	helpful	negative	reassuring	understanding
critical	honest	nervous	reflective	useful
decisive	honorable	objective	relaxed	vulnerable
demanding	humorous	observant	reliable	wise
dependable	idealistic	optimistic	religious	witty
dependent	imaginative	organized	reserved	workaholic

Which three circled words describe you the best? List them here.

1. independent
2. realistic / mature
3. determined / responsible

Now, think about activities, achievements, failures, and/or experiences that might best illustrate these adjectives. For instance, you might feel the word "caring" describes you well. When was that quality particularly evident? Perhaps you can illustrate your caring qualities by describing your feelings the time you helped your friend out of a troublesome situation, or the reasons you have a menagerie of stray animals at home.

The point here is important. Do not simply claim to possess certain qualities; you must show these qualities to your reader. In other words, when the reader is finished with the essay he or she should be thinking, "What a caring person" without you ever having to mention the word "caring."

Again, it's your turn. First, write one of the three qualities you listed:

_____independent_____

Second, provide a brief illustration of how that quality describes you:

my sister plays comp. softball.
Nearly every other weekend,
my parents leave for a
tournament. I care for myself
and my animals, get myself
_____need to go and_
_____responsibilities._
_____
_____

ıg task. Complete the following open-ended

who is always honest,
even it it is not always nice.
someone who fights for what
she wants. Someone who follows
rules.

2. During my high school days, I have succeeded at . . .

getting straight As, not
falling under peer pressure,
finding out about myself.
_____
_____
_____

3. During my high school days, I have failed at . . .

making a lot of friends,
getting really involved
in school activities/clubs.

4. The thing most often misunderstood about me is . . .

That I always get what I
want. Also, that I am mean,
when I am really just
realistic and fight for what I
want.

5. An important decision I made in high school was to . . .

get good grades and go
to a good college
right after graduation.

Do any of your answers to the above open-ended questions suggest any other potential essay topics? If so, list them below:

Maybe an important decision
I made in H.S. or
my most important traits.

Hints for Excellent Essays

1. College-essay writing follows several of the same basic principles used in your high school English classes:

   • Structure your essay so your reader (the college admission staff) gains some sense of an organized flow of ideas. Your organizational plan enables your essay to fulfill a purpose, to go someplace; it gives it a logical beginning, middle and end.

   • Write your body paragraphs first. Don't worry about your introduction until later. Normally, you should decide what you want to talk about and then make a few notes or an outline of how you will develop that topic.

   • Write a clear thesis or controlling statement.

   • Make your grammar clear and your spelling correct.

   • Make your examples specific, specific, specific. Your reader wants to know how you lost the close sailboat race, and you will help bring this to life if you describe how the boat looked and the details of the race day. Your precision should help your reader actually see the boat, the race, and the trophy. Be specific and concrete. Your essay will be interesting to read.

   • Finally, a college essay differs in one important way from an essay you might write for an expository writing class. Your college essay should *not* be written in the third person ("*one* should realize. . .") or in the second person ("if *you* are on student council. . ."). Rather, your essay should be written in the first person ("from student council, *I* learned. . ."). When you write, you should tell your reader, "I felt disappointed when I dropped the football," or "I was overjoyed when I earned an A in my very difficult math class."

2. Students often feel that negative, disappointing or uncomfortable experiences should not be used in essays. Some fear these experiences might reveal a weakness or insecurity and that such information would be a liability for an applicant. Nonsense! A sensitive, but not self-pitying, exploration and explanation of a difficult sophomore year or an uncomfortable camp experience can make a wonderful, insightful essay.

3. Write from the heart. The more effectively you can show your reader how it felt to have a car accident or make an important decision, the more your reader will know about you—and that is the goal of a good college essay. Colleges want to know about your character and your personality.

4. Students often ask how long an essay should be. While specifications on length vary (and most colleges give clear instructions), most college essays are about 250-500 words. That's less than two double-spaced, typed pages. Now, that's not so bad!

5. Perhaps the next most common question about essays is whether or not to have your English teacher or your parents read them. While English teachers can be very helpful in reading for grammatical and spelling errors as well as for some content and development issues, remember that they read as English teachers, not as admission officers, and the difference in perspective is key. Also, when parents read essays, they should not try to rephrase or restate your ideas into more complex language. Nor should they discourage you from sharing reflections about yourself that may strike your parents as revealing a weakness or an insecurity. You are human, as are admission officers, and your human insights are those that make for superior essays.

6. Finally, do not believe the lore that admission committees only read essays that are highly unusual ("a poem is really impressive" or "why don't you write your essay on the back of a photograph of your grandmother?"). If creativity or humor or poetry is you, fine. If not, do what is honestly you. Creative essays or stream of consciousness essays are acceptable if they meet the primary criterion mentioned earlier—that the essay allows the college to learn about your strengths, your motivations, and your sensitivities.

7. Okay, are you ready? Do you know the essay topic that one of your colleges lists on its application? If you completed Worksheet 10, you have, in front of you, the essay questions to which you must respond. Have you done your brainstorming? Try to formulate a thesis sentence for one of your essays. Remember, write your main points and your body paragraphs first; try writing furiously and without stopping. Try to write at least a page. Do not, at this point, censor your work. Do not stop to correct spelling or look up words online. Simply tell your story as if you were writing a letter to a friend. Then, continue writing furiously until you have completed your story. Add an interesting introductory paragraph that intrigues the reader enough to go on. Add a conclusion and voila! Obviously, you'll next want to read for grammatical and spelling errors, but you have a draft of your essay. Does it communicate? Does it say something interesting about you? Is it written honestly and with feeling? Is it completely you? If so, hooray!

Having written your essays, you may be interested in how essays fit into everything else the college reviews in making a decision on your application. The next chapter explores the dynamics of the admission process.

CHAPTER 7

■■■■■■■■■■■■■■■■■■■

THE ADMISSION PROCESS REVEALED

The process of selecting students is often cloaked in mystery and intrigue. What goes on behind the closed admission office doors? Why is one student admitted and another rejected? Surely there are some secrets which, if known, will help you get admitted. Right? Unfortunately no. What goes on in admission offices is actually not that mystical.

It is not mystical if we just think of who these people are and what their task really involves. Admission officers (Dean or Director of Admission, Director of Enrollment, Associate or Assistant Directors, Admission Counselors or Representatives) are professionals whose job it is to recruit and select both the numbers and types of students who will ultimately benefit the college. They are hired to tell the college's story to potential students and then to select, from the pool of people who submit admission applications, those students who are judged most likely to meet the goals of their college. And the goals vary widely. For some colleges, the goal is to admit students who have evidenced tremendous scholarship and who will benefit from the library holdings and the strengths of the faculty. For others, it is to enroll a freshman class large enough to allow the college to continue to expand and add new departments or programs. Most typically, colleges seek to achieve several objectives when selecting the freshman class.

Keep in mind that admission officers are human beings with a job to do. They have great sensitivity to individual differences, hence, discussions about what a college is "looking for" in a student vary tremendously. Evidence of scholarship or curiosity may mean one thing to one admission officer and something entirely different to another.

Historically, admission offices existed for the purpose of reading applications and making accept and reject decisions. In more recent years, admission offices have focused their efforts more and more on recruiting and attracting students. As a result, competition at selective institutions is more intense than ever. Admission officers who have focused on student recruitment are doing a good job—the pool of applications to their institutions is increasing—thereby enabling them to select the best qualified (in their eyes) for the spaces available in the class.

Be Yourself

Sound advice, then, is not to manipulate the admission process with gimmickry, chicanery or hocus-pocus. Such strategizing is likely to fail because colleges are well aware of the difference between genuineness and gamesmanship. Don't try to be different just for the sake of being different. There is no essay topic that always works, no perfect high school curriculum, no person whose opinion of you (via a letter of recommendation) can always sway admission committees. You may hear that you should write an essay that is creative and "far out" (and possibly even submit it on a Kleenex tissue!). You may hear that colleges "love" kids who are star athletes or do community service. You may hear that colleges really like those who take Japanese or who enroll in a summer course at a nationally known university. But none of these things is necessarily or always true.

Given that complex strategic maneuvers are of little value, how should you look at the admission process? Here are a few suggestions:

1. *Be yourself.* This may be the most important fact of all when applying to colleges. Tell your story without trying to play super-sophisticate, super-scholar or whatever. Tell your own story and *tell it well.*

2. *Make sure your course load is reflective of your best intellectual efforts.* Be realistic here also. As noted below, colleges care what classes you take and what you contribute to your classes. Take the most advanced classes you can manage without getting in over your head. Senior year is no time to slack off. Admission offices are very positive about a strong college preparatory program, with four or five solid subjects each semester. Colleges will admit you primarily on the basis of your ability to be successful doing college-level work. Show the colleges what you are capable of achieving.

3. *Do something productive with your time.* Be as constructive as you can in terms of your extracurricular activities. That arena may be creative arts or leadership or community service or work or sports or a hobby— or something else.

4. *Be informed.* Care about people and issues. Care about national or international events or happenings in your city or your school. Learn to articulate your views with reason and even with passion.

Remember the point made throughout this book: You will have good college choices if you carefully seek out those choices. Don't sit and fret because you may not get into Stanford or Swarthmore or Sewanee. If these colleges are right for you, for heaven's sake, explore them and apply if they meet *your* criteria. But if you feel that, realistically, you should not reach for the most competitive colleges, be comfortable with your choices. Many people attend lesser-known undergraduate colleges and eventually become political leaders, corporate executives, skilled doctors, lawyers, and teachers. If you must strategize, do so by finding colleges that, in fact, fit you and that will draw out the best within you.

Factors Important in Selecting Students

As indicated above, colleges use many factors to select students. Not all of those listed here are used by all colleges, but they account for most of the input into the eventual college decision. The precise blend of factors, as stated, varies by college and even by individual members of the admission staff at the same college.

1. *High school program.* The courses a student takes in high school are often, and correctly, viewed as the most important factor in selecting a freshman class. Colleges look to see what you have taken in comparison to other applicants and in comparison to what is offered at your high school. Your Admission Profile (Worksheet 4) gives you an indication of how your program compares with others. Admission officers want to see that you push yourself when choosing courses. Again, take the most challenging program (filled with honors or Advanced Placement classes and many solids during your senior year) you can handle. But know your limits as well. You want to balance the academic, extracurricular and personal sides of your life.

2. *Grades and rank-in-class.* Grades provide evidence of your capabilities and motivation. They are only significant, however, in light of your courses. Sometimes students ask if it is better to take harder classes and get lower grades or easier classes and get higher grades. Unfortunately, this question has no simple answer. Many of the most competitive colleges state that their applicants have taken the most difficult classes and received A's in them. But the answer depends on you. Surely, you should not balk at taking a more advanced class with the fear you might receive a B. Because colleges weigh these factors carefully, it is up to you to select the right program for you. Also important here are the trends in your grades over the years. Your school may or may not report your rank-in-class. If it is reported, rank gives the colleges another indication of your performance vis-a-vis others at your high school. Of course, high schools vary considerably and ranks depend upon the level of competition at your high school.

3. *Test scores.* Not all colleges view test results the same way. Some are more "test conscious" than others. An increasing number have even made the submission of test scores optional. For a listing of test-optional colleges, go to fairtest.org. By and large, test scores are viewed as important, but not as the critical variable in making an admission decision. Very large universities often place more emphasis on test scores since the numbers of applications makes thorough review of other features less likely. Most colleges count high school program difficulty and performance as more important in making admission decisions. The three entrance exams most often used by colleges are: (1) The SAT Reasoning Test (SAT); (2) The American College Test (ACT); and (3) SAT Subject Tests. Commonly, colleges require either the SAT or the ACT—rarely both. Only a few colleges require students to take the SAT Subject Tests. Colleges differ in which of these they require, and students should check application materials carefully for testing information.

4. *Extracurricular activities.* There is no such thing as the "perfect" list of extracurricular activities. Some students have exhibited extensive involvement with leadership in one or two activities. Other students have a broad set of involvements in several activities. At the most competitive colleges, accepted students have quite often achieved recognition that extends far beyond their own high school or even community; students who are recognized by their teachers and advisors as having "really made a difference." The question often asked in this area is, "what has a young person done with his or her time?" It is up to you to demonstrate, on your application, that your activities have been meaningful and noteworthy. Use Your Activities/Experiences Record, Worksheet 3, to help you think about the strength of your activities. (Worksheet 3 can also be helpful in completing your applications.) Many admission officers would prefer to see a student involved in fewer activities with evidence of sustained commitment than someone who merely joins many clubs and organizations.

5. *Personal qualities.* This factor is hard to define but it certainly plays into the admission decision. Admission officers want to know a prospective freshman as well as possible, and thus, such qualities as depth of intellectual curiosity, sustained interest in or commitment to a local or school issue, altruism, fairness, and particularly meaningful reactions to a life experience or a response to a setback can be, and often are, significant. Some students show dedication to community service,

others have special talents or abilities. Still others have travel or work experiences. Any of these may catch the eye of an admission officer. Your level of initiative in day-to-day living can be important, so can an ongoing appreciation for ethical, historical and world issues. Your college essay and the comments of teachers and others who know you, can tell the admission officer about such personal qualities.

6. *The application itself and your personal statements or essays.* Colleges today typically require students to write statements covering specific topics. Your responses to application questions, particularly essay questions, give admission officers a sense of what is important to you and how you think. As such, they become a "window to your mind." Essays were discussed in Chapter 6.

7. *Recommendations.* Most colleges require prospective freshmen to ask at least one person to complete a recommendation on his or her behalf. These recommendations are another clue to you as a person and, more importantly, you as a student. As such, give careful thought to whom you will ask to complete a recommendation form. Your best bet is those who know you well and can comment frankly on your intellectual skills as well as your potential. Frequently, your high school counselor is asked to write a recommendation for you, so get to know your counselor as well as you can. Some of the most competitive colleges also ask for teacher recommendations. Don't necessarily select the most popular teacher, the teacher who gave you your highest grade, or the teacher whom your classmates say "writes the best recommendation." Pick teachers who really know you and will take time to write insightful, thoughtful, honest letters. Because colleges are evaluating your intellectual potential through your recommendations, letters from "big wigs" such as the Governor, a leading professional in your community (who may be a graduate of the college) or other well-known persons rarely are helpful—unless that person has worked with you and can contribute something significant to your admission file. On the other hand, you should not hesitate to ask someone who knows you well—say an employer or the leader of a summer experience—to write a letter on your behalf. These letters have the potential of assisting the admission staff in knowing you. But consider your recommenders carefully. Too many recommenders can be distracting and work against you.

These are the seven factors most commonly considered by admission officers in deciding on new freshmen. But there are others. Motivation is important, as is your ability to overcome adversity. The most selective colleges seek those who are best able, by virtue of their intelligence and maturity, to use the resources—teachers, equipment, libraries, and so on— the college provides. Your level of interest in the college might also have an influence.

It is important to remember, however, that admission formulae seldom exist. Students and parents often ask, "What test score do I need to be admitted?" or "What grade point average is required for admission?" While a few (typically, those that are large and state-supported) universities actually use an admission index that consists of some combination of grades and test scores, most admission decisions are multi-faceted and, hence, hard to predict. No college ranks every applicant and then accepts a certain percentage of them. If you have completed Your Admission Profile (Worksheet 4) realistically and honestly and have read the section on "Determining Your Likelihood of Admission" in Chapter 4, you should have some sense of how you might compare with other applicants.

Behind the Scenes

Keep in mind, admission officers take all of the factors described above into consideration. Raising your test scores by, say, 100 points, does not mean your chances of getting into a very competitive college suddenly go from fair to good since your course load, grades, activities, and so on likely have not changed. Furthermore, an outstanding essay will not compensate for a weak program of classes or little evidence of commitment to academics. So while score improvements and spending time on your college essay are important, keep in mind that colleges consider the full complement of factors as they read applications for admission.

Central to this discussion is the realization that colleges admit students for many different reasons and with different admission portfolios. The most competitive colleges are seeking a diverse and "balanced" class. They seek some students because of their scholastic credentials alone and others because of what they bring to the campus in terms of unique perspectives, skills and interests. One student may be favorably considered primarily because of top grades and several involvements. Another student may be admitted because of musical or athletic talents; some hail from geographic areas underrepresented at that college.

Most very selective colleges weigh factors carefully. They may want first generation college students. They may respond favorably to sons or daughters of their alumni. The Supreme Court, in the summer of 2003, affirmed the ability of colleges to consider race as one factor in making admissions decisions. Typically, none of these qualities (alumni, geographic diversity, athletic talents, children of university employees, etc.) gets a student admitted, but they figure into the total picture and may tip the scales in favor of a particular student.

As such, it is significant to remember that admission decisions are not, by definition, fair and equitable. Why? Because they are human and, thus, subjective. What may grab the attention of one admission officer may not even raise the brow of another one. How one college elects to balance a class may be different from how another college does it. Further, the relative weight of test scores, essays or extracurricular activities varies widely from one college to the next—even among colleges perceived as similar in their level of admission difficulty.

As an applicant, then, your best game plan is to approach the college choice process realistically. As stated before, you do have choices and you should concentrate on colleges where you will "fit in." "Fitting in" is still more important than "getting in." In terms of "getting in," you should focus on colleges where you perceive you have a reasonable chance of admission. Sure, have one or two "reach" colleges (where your chance of admission is less, but still possible) but spend the majority of your time on those schools where your background and skills suggest a good chance of admission. Don't become unglued because there are a few colleges where you will likely not be admitted. As stated in Chapter 1, be happy because over 2,500 colleges do want you! Success in college is what really counts.

Dealing with Admission Decisions: Accept, Reject and Wait List

The end of the college planning process involves making the decision of which college you will attend. Part of that decision may have been made for you . . . by the colleges to which you applied. Your thoroughness likely has led to appropriate college choices, and acceptance letters from colleges that really fit and where you can make a contribution. If so, congratulations are in order. The sequence of events discussed in the next several paragraphs frequently occurs in February, March and April of your Senior year.

Before you receive decision letters from your colleges, you need to think about your priority list. What school is your first choice? Second choice? As you know, the process of college planning involved considering high-, medium- and low-chance of admission schools. Even if you haven't visited your schools and, based solely on your research, which is your favorite high-chance school? Medium-chance? Low-chance? Talk to your parents about your choices. What schools do they like for you? Why?

Acceptance Letters

You will receive one of three letters from colleges; an acceptance, a rejection or a wait list notification. If you are offered admission, congratulations! You may want to visit or revisit the schools you are accepted to in order to finalize your decision. No schools require you to provide a housing deposit before May 1st, but with big state schools (where housing may be tight), one should assure housing early. Finally, as soon as you know where you want to go, be sure to send in your deposit. But don't forget to keep your grades up as schools have been known to retract their offer if the student's grades fall significantly. Also, you should send a letter to other schools that have accepted you (letting them know your decision); it's the right thing to do.

Rejection Letters

If the letter you receive is a rejection, you will feel disappointed. A denial letter hurts, and nothing said here is likely to ease the pain. It is tempting to suggest that the college is really not the best fit and your other choices are more appropriate. It is also tempting to say that the admission process is sometimes unfair and that good students are often left without an acceptance while others, perceived as less well qualified, have gained admission. Both of these temptations, while perhaps truthful, miss the true feelings that are present whenever such a setback hits. What is true is this: Never has admission to college been as difficult as in the last few years. Furthermore, admission is a subjective and sometimes unpredictable process. Admission directors often state that the process is imprecise, subjective and seldom reflective of who will be most successful in life.

While it is practically impossible not to take a letter of rejection personally, the truth is: what drives selective admission decisions today is what the college needs, not what any individual applicant possesses. Don't let a college admission office dictate your worth as a student or as an individual. The most important thing is to rally and move forward quickly. Arrange to visit schools and be prepared to make a decision by May 1. Reactions to such setbacks distinguish a person with character and grit from those who whine and lack moral strength. Your ability to handle a denial with guts says a great deal about you as a person and as a successful college student, wherever you decide to attend.

The Wait List

Finally, you may receive a letter offering you a place on the wait list. This is the most complex alternative because it is so tenuous and uncertain and it is difficult, indeed typically impossible, to predict the outcome. The number of people accepted off the wait list varies dramatically from school to school and from year to year. If you are placed on a waiting list:

1. Remain calm. This is an important decision-making time and approaching things rationally is critical.

2. It is imperative that you evaluate the schools to which you were offered admission and decide which of them you want to attend. It is not feasible or appropriate to wait to hear from the wait list college(s) before deciding. Indeed, most schools don't know if they will have a space until well after May 1. Some students feel a college is "better" if it wait listed them instead of admitting them. Please accept the reality of the situation:
If a student applies to two equal colleges, one might accept and the next might wait list (or reject). It has no relevance to academic excellence of the colleges OR to finding a good match for you. Visit these accepted schools, again if necessary, and decide where you will attend. When you decide, pay a deposit to secure your place for the fall.

3. At the same time, if you feel the school is a good enough match for you, "pursue the waitlist." Think if there are ways to demonstrate your continuing interest in the school. Two ideas to consider are: (1) sending a letter of continued interest and (2) sending your most current grades (if outstanding). Speak to your high school counselor about these and other options.

No college is perfect and while it's easy to "coronate" a college or university as the *perfect* place, the truth, as has been stated many times in this book, is that there are wonderful opportunities awaiting you at many colleges. Hopefully you will be accepted at your first choice school, but if you are not, it is important to put all of this in perspective, rebound, and make your college years, wherever you attend, meaningful and successful.

The next chapter focuses on the important skills, perception and attitudes that lead to that successful freshman year.

Chapter 8

■■■■■■■■■■■■■■■■■■■

Being Successful
in Your Freshman Year

Beginning your collegiate experience may bring on a number of emotions: enthusiasm and fear are two of the most common. You may feel enthusiasm because you are beginning a new chapter in your life. This new chapter may allow you to continue a successful high school career and reach new heights. Or it may allow you the opportunity for a fresh start with people who don't have any preconceived notions about your potential. You may feel fear because college is a new experience and new experiences are often approached with a certain amount of trepidation and uncertainty. You will be leaving your familiar surroundings and entering a community that will present new people, new circumstances and new stresses.

It is important to remember that you will always need to balance your study and academic-success needs with your fun and relationship needs. Successful college students know—or, more commonly, learn to know— how to do that. But it takes time to make a complete adjustment. Some argue that you need a full year of college to make a total adjustment.

This Chapter is designed to give you a few pointers that may help contribute to success in college. But there are no easy answers; no recipe will "cook up" a successful college career for you. Because everyone is different, some of the following ideas may be valuable to you; others may not be. Use what you find helpful as you approach the challenges and excitement of your freshman year.

Attitudes

1. Make a commitment to succeed. It sounds so simple, but often, at the heart of unsuccessful college students is a lack of commitment to academic success.

2. Make academic success your top priority. No one can do that for you. There will be plenty of time for fun, but your obligation, first and foremost, is to your intellectual development and growth.

3. Don't sit back waiting for the college to be "exciting." You make it happen. Get out. Meet new people. Get involved. College, like life, is what you make it.

4. Remember that there will always be ups and downs during your college years. During big changes in our lives (such as starting college) our emotions can become exaggerated. Give things time to fall into place. Allow time to get to know people. Most students are not able to fully evaluate their college experience until the spring of their freshman year. There will always be good days and bad days, good experiences and lousy ones. On your bad days, learn to relax, maintain your equilibrium and move forward. Don't let one low grade (or, more likely, a negative comment from your roommate) throw you into a tailspin.

5. Anticipate homesickness. You have left your home, your family and your friends. You will miss them. Don't try to pretend homesickness is not there. Experiencing homesickness does not suggest weakness. Share your feelings with others and maintain regular contact with home. And bring a piece of home with you—pictures of friends and family, your yearbook, posters, etc.

6. Learn to tolerate some degree of bureaucracy. Be prepared for the runaround. Ask two or three people the same question before you are certain of an answer.

7. Be ready to tolerate a lack of privacy. Residence hall rooms are often small, and cramped spaces can mean short fuses. Use your space wisely. Live in your room but also find a way to live outside of your room by going to the library, the dorm lounge, or the student center.

8. Stand up for your own values and preferences. Don't succumb to peer pressure. Be true to your self. People respect those with conviction.

9. Think about the type of person you want to be in college. The high school you may be different from the college you. Do you want to be known as a scholar? Leader? Follower? Person with values? Bystander? Party Animal? It is up to you to make these choices.

10. Before leaving for college, talk with your parents and friends about how they see your adjustment in the first few weeks of college. How do they feel you will react to a new and unknown situation? Such insights from those you know and respect can help improve your chances for a smooth transition.

Academics

1. Seek help immediately if you feel you don't understand a particular class. With only a few graded assignments per term, waiting to see how you do on the next test (or paper) may be too late. It's up to you. There will not be any calls home, progress reports, etc. You need to stay on top of your work. Many professors are slightly subjective graders and the more you meet with them, the more likely they are to remember you come grading time.

2. Work hard to get good grades from the beginning of your college days. A low grade point average after one semester puts tremendous pressure on you later.

3. Meet with professors! Schedule an appointment or drop by and introduce yourself during their posted office hours. And find at least one professor during your freshman year with whom you feel comfortable talking to about the ins and outs of the school, your career, etc.

4. It is important to go to class! Research studies show that academic success is as dependent on class attendance as on the amount of time spent studying.

5. Teachers are people, too! If you've enjoyed a class, tell the instructor. Keep in touch with teachers or administrators you like. They can become friends who will 'show you the ropes' and can possibly help you later with a recommendation for a job or for graduate school.

6. Select your courses well, but don't be afraid to drop a course if it is too much for you. The ability to drop a class is a major benefit to college. However, learn the official college procedures for dropping classes and follow them or you may wind up with an "F" on your record.

Using Resources

1. Remember, being independent doesn't mean you have to do everything yourself. Seek help when you need it.

2. Speak up. Don't let course difficulties, roommate problems, homesickness, etc., back you into a corner. Let someone know. Take action. Colleges are filled with people who are paid to help you. For example:

   • The Counseling Center for homesickness, test anxiety, relationship problems, and general adjustment difficulties.

   • The Dean of Students office for questions about getting involved in activities and general questions about how the college operates.

- Your Resident Advisor or Resident Assistant for help with roommates, excessive dorm noise, homesickness and suggestions for meeting people and getting involved.
- A Peer Counselor for help and support with college adjustment and advice about good professors.
- Your Academic Advisor for advice about your schedule, classes, work load, choice of major, and career ideas.
- The Health Center for a throat culture, a prescription, care of physical ailments or for counseling.
- Religious Services, Chaplaincy for personal concerns and spiritual strength.
- The Financial Aid office for information on scholarships, loans or work opportunities.

3. Talk to juniors and seniors who "know the ropes." They know good professors and how to handle the bureaucracy. Ask for suggestions.

Courses, Majors and Careers

1. Be patient. Don't come unglued if you listed mathematics as your major on your application and now as a freshman you are certain you do not want to major in math. Freshman programs are typically quite similar; that is, most freshmen students take general courses required for graduation. Discuss the fact that you are not sure about your major with your advisor and sign up for classes that are required of all students. During your first year you need not worry too much about picking a major.

2. Make a distinction between "major" and "career." A major is an academic field you like and want to learn more about. A career is the lifework you choose to pursue after college. Many students who ultimately go on to medical school choose undergraduate majors in English or French; lots of students who go on to graduate business school choose undergraduate majors in chemistry or philosophy. Take courses that will maximize your chances of success.

3. Don't feel compelled to make a career choice immediately. Again, be patient. Sample lots of courses and disciplines. Actively explore potential career possibilities. Take advantage of opportunities for part-time jobs or internships in career fields of interest. Also ask teachers about job opportunities in their subject areas and use the career planning office for an interest assessment and for information.

Other People

1. Anticipate different lifestyles. Be ready to communicate with your roommate to resolve problems. Remember, learning to resolve conflicts with roommates and others can be a good start to honing your ability to resolve other "people problems" in life. Be open when it comes to differences—and willing to learn. You may have to negotiate some issues by talking about them. Don't hold your feelings inside; express them with tact and consideration. Find other friends in addition to your roommate.

2. Try not to be intimidated by all the new people. Don't be afraid of all the differences—socio-economic, family, religion, opinion—you will encounter. View these differences as opportunities to broaden your horizons and be open to them. You may find you have more in common with other students than you first thought. Remember, everyone is new, not just you. Capitalize on this and make lots of friends.

3. When you find yourself in a group of people and you feel uncomfortable, realize that other people in the group feel exactly the same way. Introduce yourself to someone you do not know. Ask that person some questions. Begin and continue a conversation. Work at listening and accepting others; the first step to being accepted yourself is to accept others.

4. Remember, new friends can't immediately fill the gap left by separation from long-standing friendships. Be patient.

5. Share your goals with your roommate or others you trust. Say to your roommate, "I'm working toward a 3.0 this semester. I need your help in achieving this goal." Openness, cooperation and sharing help you achieve your goals.

6. Don't eat alone. Introduce yourself to someone.

Controlling Time

1. Time flies faster in college than it ever has. Keep this in mind and plan out each day. Know how long things take to accomplish.

2. Time is the one commodity everyone in college possesses equally. Students who use those 24 hours wisely are typically the ones who end up successful.

3. One student's schedule for accomplishing tasks may not resemble another's. You need to know yourself and your work pace well enough to be able to determine about how long it takes you to write a five-page paper or read 50 pages. Allow enough time to get your work done.

4. Keep up with your assignments each day. Most often, college students are not given assignments on a daily basis. Rather, you will get assignments for an entire term. It's up to you to determine what needs to be done daily so you will not be cramming for midterms or finals.

5. Utilize the library and other relatively quiet places on campus to study. You'll get more done in a shorter time than in your dorm room. Sometimes even getting away from your computer or your phone for a few hours can re-energize you for studying.

6. Try to get as much studying done during the day as possible because at night it can be hard to tell friends you can't go out with them.

7. Understand the extent of your scheduled hours. Scheduled hours are those over which you have no control, for example, class time, team practice time, and dining hall hours. Knowing your scheduled hours will help you plan your unscheduled hours (such as studying, sports, texting, spending time on the computer, phoning, and being with friends).

8. Allow yourself enough time for sleep. This may sound silly and unnecessary, but college students are prone to wear themselves out by not sleeping enough.

9. Discipline your time by balancing study sessions with social outings. Learn to say "no." You may need to say, "I'm not going to the party tonight because I'm going to study." There will always be another party. There will not be another chance for a successful freshman year.

10. Plan your study schedule carefully. For completing major tasks, one or two hours of concentrated time is better than one or two hours of interrupted time. You should discover when and where such concentrated time is possible.

11. Know where your time is going. You may be surprised to find that your time usage is not what you think it is—or ought to be. TV, cards, computer, Blackberry, iPhone, texting, a romance, etc. can take up HOURS of time.

12. Keep a calendar. Note important academic dates—when tests are scheduled, when papers are due, and so on. On long term projects, like a term paper, break the assignment up into small segments and establish your own due dates along the way. For example, what is your goal (due date) for finishing the background reading? For writing the first draft? List all of these dates on your calendar. By working steadily on long projects, you will avoid having to do all the work in one night.

13. Limit your time online. Hours can go by while you are instant messaging, playing games, answering e-mails, etc. Know your priorities.

Other Areas

1. Your personal safety on campus is your responsibility. Urban or rural, large or small, crimes occur on every campus. Be careful about where and when you walk at night, about keeping your room locked and about being accountable for your personal belongings. Do not expect the college to be responsible for you or your possessions.

2. Participate in extracurricular activities. Studies show that the more "connected" you are to a college, the more fun and successful your experience will be. Connectedness most often comes from a commitment to a group or an organization. Think about two or three activities you want to explore when you arrive on campus. Remember, however, that your activities should be somewhat limited your first year—particularly if you are concerned about your ability to stay on top of your studies. Academics do come first.

3. What if you don't get into your first choice fraternity or sorority? What if you don't make the tennis team? Such experiences can initially be devastating, but, again deal with your hurt and move on. Learning to overcome or deal with setbacks can be a valuable life skill. Find other groups to join and other ways to use your out-of-class time.

4. Carefully consider whether the electronics you bring with you (iPods, TVs, Playstations, Wiis, computers, etc.) can give you an excuse to be a hermit. You'll only find extracurricular activities when you seek them out.

5. Don't be wrapped up in trying to have the 'typical college experience.' There are many different types of college experiences depending on who you are and where you are going to college. Your experience may differ from your parents or your friends at other schools.

6. Keep a journal of your college years. It is amazing how much you will do and how much of it you can forget.

7. Stay in touch with your parents. They care about you and will be grateful if you share your collegiate experiences with them.

College is a wonderful time of your life. It is filled with new experiences, new ideas and new discoveries. Your success in college is not a function of your high school grades or your SAT/ACT scores. It is a function of your determination, motivation, organization and ability to handle new situations. Go for it.

The next chapter focuses on the important role your parents play in your college decision-making. While it is written for your parents, you should read it as well. It may enable you to see the college planning process from their point of view and provide perspectives on some of the issues you may be talking about at home.

CHAPTER 9

■■■■■■■■■■■■■■■■■■■

PARENTS AS EDUCATORS IN THE
COLLEGE SELECTION PROCESS

The process of identifying, researching, and ultimately selecting a college should involve the entire family, and throughout this book, students have been encouraged to discuss their thinking with their parents. While the rest of this book has been written for the student, this chapter is written for parents. So the *you* in this chapter refers to parents!

College admission in the 21st century is very different than it was when you considered colleges. The population of students seeking admission has exploded and the nature of college selection itself has changed dramatically. The history of college admission is beyond the scope of this book, but it is interesting to note that, in 1932, 1,300 students applied to Yale and over 70% were admitted. Of these, many graduated from elite, Eastern preparatory schools and about one-fourth were sons of Yale graduates. Today, Yale receives applications from about 20,000 students per year and admits less than 10%. Further, admittees come from a wide range of high schools and are diverse in multiple ways. Due to these changes, your role as the parent of a college-bound student is a difficult one. You must consider so many issues, emotions, and contradictory advice. Some parents feel as overwhelmed as their sons and daughters. But, like the student, you should approach this college-seeking process with systematic persistence. Move, with your child, through the various stages of choosing a college as they are presented in this book.

Your role as counselor, advisor, and helper will aid your prospective college student in growing and learning through this process, however, students must take the lead. They should seek your advice and help, but they must be responsible for the decision. If a parent takes over the process of choosing, the student doesn't learn. If the parent is excessively anxious, the student will act likewise.

You want your son or daughter to make a good decision, and you have worked hard over the years to enable your young person to attend college.

Be clear about your expectations, but give students the room they need to contemplate the issues they face in choosing a college and in making the right decision. Someone once made a good point when saying, "I've been working with this age group for some years now and I've learned they're a lot like flowers: they need nurturing but they also need to be left alone."

Commonly Asked Questions

Let's begin by discussing seven common questions from parents as they and their students begin to think about college.

Question 1—My daughter can't plan for college. She doesn't even know what she wants to study! Is it important for my daughter to know what she wants to do in life?

While this concern is common and well-intentioned, parents and students must view college planning as a process significantly different from career planning. In the truest sense, the undergraduate years are intended as a time for self-discovery and intellectual discovery. One of the best ways of selecting an eventual course of study (a major) and/or a career is by identifying subjects and classes in which a student has interest and by discovering those intellectual and personal talents or gifts that each student possesses. While it is difficult for a high school senior to make the leap from identifying favorite subjects to identifying a career path, let your daughter's likes and dislikes play a role in her initial major selection. But keep in mind, an art major can wind up in medical school and an English literature major can become a clinical psychologist.

Hence, you should set aside (at least for now) any concerns you have about your daughter's lack of career direction. If she has no idea about potential careers, she may want to look at colleges that offer a broad range of academic programs (a liberal arts and sciences emphasis) so she can keep her options open while making a decision. On the other hand, if she has a sense for what she would like to study, that's great too. Remember, though, the typical college student changes his or her major at least twice during a four-year college program. What is important is that your daughter *actively* explore different career possibilities during her undergraduate years. This is accomplished by taking a wide variety of courses, asking teachers about vocations in their fields, participating in internships, using vacations for work experiences in career areas of interest, and utilizing the resources (such as the career planning office) available on college campuses.

By the way, many colleges ask students to declare a major field on their admission application. If your daughter remains undecided, she should choose a subject of interest without feeling as though she's locking herself into a definitive career path.

Question 2—We want our son to attend a college we've heard of—after all, when he gets out in the "real world," the name of his alma mater will be the ticket to employment. Right?

Not necessarily. This question can be answered on two levels. First, as mentioned in Chapter 1, the United States has approximately 4,000 colleges. Name recognition varies by area and industry. In other words, parents living in Connecticut employed by the hospitality industry will likely recognize a different set of colleges than will parents living in New Mexico employed by the aerospace industry. Oh, but you ask, aren't the Ivy League colleges the "best?" Wouldn't any prospective employer give an absolute edge to an Ivy League grad? No, on both counts. First, a college's membership in the Ivy League Athletic Conference is no guarantee of academic or social fit for any given student; most importantly, though, perceptions among potential employers about any given college are almost as variable as the employers themselves. We know of no study that has determined Ivy League graduates have a lock on names of the most wealthy persons in our society. Or the most powerful. Or the most humanitarian.

Increasingly, as mentioned earlier, employers are interested in knowing what any given student has "done" at his or her college. Academic success is reflected by grades, research, independent study, study abroad, honors, and special projects. Social success is evidenced by leadership, participation, and commitments to activities, people, and projects. In the end, these accomplishments matter far more than the name of the school a student lists on a resume. Significantly, a study supported by the U.S. Department of Education found that the name or prestige of the college a student attends has very little influence on future earning potential. "What you do in college does make a big difference," the study reported. In fact, evidence published by Terenzini and Pascarella, in their book, *How College Affects Students,* suggests that only 1 to 2 percent of the differences in income after graduation are attributable to the specific college a student attends. But, you ask, won't the name of a college open doors and create contacts for my son? Yes, that is probably true. Friendships formed in college are likely to be lifelong. Yet, every college has an alumni network accessible to its new graduates. So, to answer the question directly, doors are open to those who achieve at a high level in college—help your son pick the college that will facilitate that achievement and result in feelings of accomplishment.

In a recent year, New York University had 37,000 applications for a freshman class of 4,300. The University of California, Los Angeles (UCLA) received over 44,000 applications for a recent freshman class. It admits less than 25% of those who apply and is even more competitive for those living outside of California. More specifically, UCLA (a selective school, but not among the most choosy) admitted only 50% of those with SAT math scores above 700 and/or ACT composite scores over 30. Pushing for a big name college (public or private), in this day of intense competition among the most competitive colleges, often leads to tears. Even worse, it takes the emphasis away from the appropriate focus of college planning: Where will a young person be successful and happy in his or her undergraduate years?

Question 3—We want our daughter to go to a "better" school than we did. Are we wrong?

No, and this concern is well-intentioned. Some parents' college decisions were actually made for them, either by their own parents ("you will go to the local college!") or because of finances ("we simply can't afford another school") or because college choices were simply not known. Furthermore, there was not the same perception that college selection involved choice. (The age of information and marketing has made college options and the information about them increase at an explosive rate.) So, looked at one way, this third question may revolve around the way parents made their own college decisions. Share with your daughter how you decided to attend the college that you did. If you did not attend college, talk with your daughter about your thoughts and dreams when you left high school.

Another aspect of this question relates to issues of prestige and goals that you may have for your daughter. Some parents so burden their children with their own unfulfilled dreams that they pressure their children into considering prestigious colleges so that they themselves will be perceived positively. Please have dreams and goals for your daughter. Share those dreams with her, and distinguish them from your own aspirations. Be careful that your student uses your perceptions only as information in the formulation of her own unique goals and aspirations. Help your daughter discover and name her talents and gifts and then point her in directions that will give her opportunities to develop. Also, work to respect the differences between you and your daughter. Do not assume your wonderful experience at a particular type of college will fit your daughter as well.

The appropriate college choice for your young person is that college where she will be able to enjoy success—an important ingredient in the development of self-esteem. Remember, it is your daughter, not you, who will spend hours and days in the classroom and in the library. Help her make those hours enjoyable and rewarding, not filled with struggle, frustration and tears, simply because she made a college decision for you, not herself.

Finally, once your daughter does make a college decision, affirm her choice. Spare her from feeling guilty if she happens to make a choice that would not be yours. Help her know her choices are acceptable to you. A college choice is rarely "right" or "wrong" in the abstract. In fact, it is clear to those advising young people in college choice that adolescents really do know what is best for themselves. They will tell us, if only we will listen.

Question 4—Our son hasn't been too successful in high school, so we don't want to spend very much for his college education. Wouldn't we just be throwing money down the drain?

At its core, this concern views the amount of money spent on college tuition as a reward or punishment for performance. While practicality may suggest this position is logical, parents are advised to view the college experience not as a product with a price tag affixed, but rather as a process whose benefits are without price. An inexpensive college is no more likely to provide a successful college experience for a late bloomer than an expensive one. The most important concern should be your son's match to the college and the ability of the college environment to provide the qualities and people necessary for your son to succeed.

Question 5—How do I deal with images and perceptions about colleges?

There are so many images about colleges, and the grapevine seems to continue to work overtime! Here are a few perceptions; some stated seriously, some stated humorously:

"Only a big school can be fun."

"The best colleges are in the East."

"Without fraternities and sororities, my son won't have a social life."

"The College of the Sun is a party school."

Students can have a great deal of fun at a small school; many would even contend that the *absence* of fraternities and sororities is a guarantee of a social life. No school is entirely a party school, nor is any school entirely a grind school. Students will surely find parties and grinds at every school if they seek those kinds of experiences.

"The College of the Urbanites is dangerous because it is located in a city."

"My daughter will have nothing to do at The University of the Ruralites because it is located in a small town."

A city is not a city is not a city (with apologies to Gertrude Stein); in short, not every urban campus is dangerous, nor every small town a bore. Small towns across the country vary a great deal, so also do the colleges located in them.

Sometimes perceptions are based on experience and sometimes they are based on hearsay or outdated notions. Verify what you hear with reliable information. Be wary of blanket statements about any given school or area of the country. And be cautious about accepting such stereotypes from your son or daughter.

Question 6—Admission decisions seem so irrational and unpredictable. What's going on?

Admission is a complex though not mystical process. Rarely does one factor, like SAT or ACT scores, an average letter of recommendation, or one low grade, in and of itself, cause a student to be denied or accepted. As described in Chapter 7, admission committees carefully and thoughtfully consider many dimensions of each applicant when they admit a class and it is difficult to predict who will get into one school from one year to the next. Hence, the fact that one student was admitted one year with particular SAT scores means very little for admission of another student with another set of scores the following year. More importantly, many factors are considered. Be cautious of parents who talk about SATs, grade point averages, etc. of students who gained or were denied admission to certain colleges. Again, the grapevine at work! Students and parents seldom know all the details contained in another student's admission folder.

Further, the admission picture for any given school changes from year to year depending on the number of applications received for the freshman class and the qualities of the class that are sought. Most importantly, we do not know whether the college that matched a student's friend also matches the needs of your student. Importantly, too, parents should work hard to assess their student objectively in light of the criteria available from most counselors. The Admission Profile, Worksheet 4, can help you compare your student with others.

While every parent would like to believe that his or her son or daughter is simply tops (and should be in your eyes), admission committees see a young person inevitably in light of the other thousands of applications they read each year. Remember, the U.S. has over 20,000 high schools, each with a valedictorian. Many of those 20,000 valedictorians apply to the 100 most selective colleges in the nation. Further, it is increasingly common for students to have over 700 on the critical reading and the math sections of the SAT and, in this day of grade inflation, thousands of students have perfect 4.0 grade point averages.

Question 7—My daughter's counselor can't tell us what the precise requirements are for admission at a particular college. Shouldn't he know if the college requires, say, a 3.2 grade average and a combined critical reading and mathematics (SAT) score of 1200?

Few colleges admit by a strict formula. Most colleges weigh all the factors discussed in Chapter 7 in making admission decisions, for example, strength of the student's program, recommendations, test scores, activities, and evidence of intellectual curiosity. Your counselor, however, should be able to give you some indication of your daughter's admission chances based on her or his experience with other students applying to that college. You, too, can assess your student's chances by reading the section titled "Concerning Your Likelihood of Admission" in Chapter 4.

Your Proper Level of Involvement

Choosing a college is a family decision, with the student in the driver's seat. In fact, parents ought to look on the college admission and decision-making process as an educational opportunity. A student who makes a college decision makes one of the most critical decisions in his or her life. Like most decisions, it should be made strategically and systematically, not serendipitously or whimsically.

Unfortunately, many students come to the college decision with little or no experience at major decision-making. Hence, parents do their young people a very valuable service by illustrating and giving them practice at making small choices. Parents aid their students by giving them strategies for solving problems but then allowing them to take the lead in the college admission process. Students, not parents, should arrange college visits, request applications and catalogues and, of course, be responsible for their own applications and essays and personal statements. Help your young person be organized, but leave it up to him or her to establish an application timetable and meet deadlines. Yes, the process seems confusing and is, at best, complex. Each college may have a different application deadline and request different documents. And even if a student can make sense out of these issues, he or she is not guaranteed admission.

Nevertheless, the planning process presents a number of opportunities for students to learn leadership and control. Importantly, too, in the context of

college planning, students will gradually move from dependence to independence. And when students do not assume control, or when they slip, you
can help most by *not* rescuing them! Instead of taking over the process, talk
through strategies with your student. Help your student learn how to
address new problems as they arise. After all, once fall arrives and college
registration is complete, a young person will not have a parent available at
every turn or at every disappointment. Instead, they will call upon the
problem-solving skills you have taught them, and be empowered to make
decisions on their own.

For a selection of college planning resources geared to parents, check the
"Parent Guides" section of the References for College Planning at the end
of the book. Coburn and Treeger's book, *Letting Go*, is the best known.
Another is *Admission Matters* by Springer and Franck. Thacker's *College
Unranked* is useful and, while not specifically about college, *The Paradox
of Choice*, by Schwartz, has valuable commentary about choices generally.

College Parents (collegeparents.com) might be of interest for links to
things like fraternity hazing, money management, etc. For data on campus
safety and security, go to ope.ed.gov/security/search.asp.

The college decision is also a decision about familial values. Is a religious
environment really best for your daughter? How important is college cost?
Is it critical that your son be near relatives so he can celebrate major
holidays with extended family? Would you pay more for a college you
perceive as higher in status? The questions and the issues are endless. Most
families leave their values unstated; the college decision-making process
can change that. By working with your student on Worksheets 5 and 6
you'll find ample opportunities to discuss the values and beliefs your family
unit views as important.

Trust, openness and supportiveness are key qualities that help ease the
college planning process. Permit your young person to try out ideas and
plans on you without reacting in horror. It is common for students to have a
different favorite college or major each week of the senior year! A student
may even claim he or she is not going to go to college—often this feeling
simply reflects their exasperation and anxiety over gathering information
and making an important decision. Again, the best response is to provide an
arena for a calm discussion of strategies; in the case of the young person
who indicated he was not going to college, his mother engaged him in a
discussion of the pros and cons of two alternatives—going to college or
taking a year off to work..

Emotions like fear, frustration, defensiveness, and anger may arise during
the college planning process. By applying to college, your young person is,

perhaps for the first time, holding up his or her credentials against the light of a wider base than that provided by the home high school. And putting oneself against a new background of competition often leads to fear and uncertainty. At the same time that your adolescent is making a very important decision, he or she is also deciding to leave the supportive and familiar environment of home and family. In preparing for college, a student is initiating action that causes separation and often pain. It is no surprise, then, that some students are ambivalent and procrastinate about completing their applications and, ultimately about making a decision on which college to attend. Also, it is no wonder that some feel defensive and want to be fiercely independent (gaining some early practice before leaving home). Each of these reactions is normal, human and, frankly, quite understandable. While these reactions may tax the patience and the tempers of parents, empathy and understanding will go a long way in keeping peace at home during the senior year. The year before college is one of the most poignant times for parents as they must balance their roles of separation and support. Remember, no single way of accomplishing these tasks is "best" or "right."

Some Specific Suggestions

The previous pages dealt with broad issues and questions. But some specific suggestions may help summarize and condense the important college planning issues for parents.

1. Assist your young person in keeping track of the college planning goals provided in Appendices A, B and C.

2. Few parents, no matter how intelligent or professionally successful, know a lot about colleges. Further, just "having time" is not the most important quality in helping your student. Trust your counselor and heed his or her advice. Attend programs held at your high school concerning college planning and meet with the college counselor.

3. Encourage your son or daughter to appraise objectively his or her abilities and limitations. Consider such questions as: In which subjects does your young person excel? At what level are his or her high school classes? Which subjects are most difficult? How are his or her study skills? How well does he or she communicate, orally as well as on paper? What is your young person's experience in such classes as English, mathematics, laboratory sciences, foreign languages? How are his or her college entrance test scores?

4. Assist your student in assessing interests and preferences. Ask questions such as: About which subjects is your student passionate? What does he

or she read for pleasure? What hobbies does he or she pursue? In which extracurricular activities has your student found the most enjoyment? Which jobs have been most interesting?

5. Help your student sort out the most important qualities in his or her choice of college (by reviewing Worksheets 5 and 6). As you review these qualities, you will want to arrive at consensus with your student about such issues as cost, size, distance from home and religious affiliation. The best college decision you can help your young person make is one that represents the best match of a student's interests, abilities, preferences, and unique qualities with the characteristics and special features of any given college. The most critical consideration is choosing an academic environment in which your young person will thrive, mature, and find enjoyment as well as stimulation.

6. Be a careful, systematic, and thoughtful aid in the information-gathering and decision-making processes. Help your student use the resources listed in Chapter 4. Colleges do a lot of aggressive marketing, and while students may feel flattered by receiving all their mail and phone calls, do not overinterpret the intent of the communication. But recognize that at some point you stop gathering *facts* and begin gathering *feelings*.

7. Encourage your son or daughter to keep his or her options open and to have many college choices. Don't focus on one college too early in the process. Your son or daughter should have colleges at each level of admission selectivity. There should be at least one college where admission chances are high, one with "medium" admission chances and one "reach" college (where admission chances are lower). Each of these colleges should be fully acceptable to you. See Chapter 4 for ways of identifying these admission categories. You can be most helpful in the application completion phase (in the Fall of the Senior year) by encouraging your student to establish a target date for each application and by urging systematic completion of applications (for example, complete one application per weekend for a month). Worksheet 10 in Chapter 4 will help keep track of application steps.

8. No college is perfect. Parents can help each student evaluate how he or she will cope with the inherent trade-offs among the good and bad features of each school.

9. Share with your student your own feelings, thoughts, and expectations about college but label them as such. Use your adult maturity and objectivity to be open-minded and nonjudgmental as you listen to your child. Avoid the "my sister-in-law's cousin's daughter said college Z is horrible" mentality.

10. Encourage your student to share his or her thoughts, feelings, and ideas about college. Talk about fears such as an admission denial, homesickness and how you will communicate when he or she is away from home.

11. Respect your student's desires for privacy about his or her scores, grades, and other pertinent admission information. The stress and uncertainty of college planning often brings parents of students into contact with each other, and discussions about the frustrations and excitement of college planning can be beneficial. Your student's specific scores and grade point average, however, are confidential and only he or she may choose to share them with others.

12. Be aware of the language you use as you talk about college plans to others. Avoid saying *"We* are looking at small colleges," or *"We've* decided to attend State U." Your student is the one making the college choice; the plural pronoun, "we," is inappropriate and pulls the focus away from the central figure in the process, your student.

13. Finally, don't be tempted to think that advances in technology have made planning for college different than it was 20 years ago. Yes, there are cell phones and iPods and instant messaging, but the uncertainty of leaving home and the need for your love remains.

Dealing With Rejection

Good college planning suggests that a student's application list should contain at least one or two "reach" schools where the likelihood of admission is slim—perhaps as low as 10-20%. Of course, the application list should also include a group of schools where the likelihood of admission (as discussed in Chapter 4) is much higher. In short, then, good counseling anticipates rejection. Information on admission decisions, including wait lists, and more thoughts about college-denial letters is found at the end of Chapter 7.

Any admission denial is disappointing, and parents can help their students understand that "rejection" from a college does not mean rejection as a person. A denial usually means a college simply had too many applications for the available spaces in its dormitories, or that the college felt (based on its experience and judgment) the student would likely not have a successful experience there.

A rejection can shatter a teenager's confidence. If expanded and repeated, it can do major damage to a student's sense of self-worth. The denial comes at a particularly difficult time in a teenager's life, a time when he or she is struggling with such issues as independence, confidence and self-worth.

The acceptance is seen not only as an admission to college, but as admission to future success and ultimate happiness. Indeed, students may see acceptance to a prestigious university as a mark of value and worthiness. Do not let a college decision become a part of self-image. Also, parents can help by pointing out that admission decisions are often subjective and impersonal. Be disappointed for your student and with your student, not because of your student. Decisions reflect human judgments, and human judgments can never be infallible. For all the information colleges have about any applicant, many bits of information remain unassessed; for example, schools cannot easily quantify or evaluate motivation, creativity, and kindness. Help your student know that regardless of the decisions made by colleges, he or she is inherently and completely acceptable.

If your student is not admitted to his or her first choice, recognize the feelings your young person is facing. Dealing with setbacks is never easy, but parental attitudes play a major role in a student's emotional well-being during this period. Encourage your son or daughter to bounce back and make the most of his or her number two college choice. Since success in college is extremely important, persuade your young person to take advantage of the opportunities available at his or her second choice. Getting top grades, making a real contribution to a campus community and developing his or her people-skills will go a long way toward employment opportunities or graduate school acceptances after four years.

All students are acceptable! But if a student does receive an admission denial, parents will do well to help their student understand that such a letter is not the end of the world. Keep the process in perspective and affirm the worth of your child.

Final Comments

Parents, your role in the process of helping your young person select a college is central and important. You will set the stage on which a crucial decision will take place. Your insights and your emotional level-headedness will contribute to the final choice.

Parents can help their students through the college choice process by promoting their children's self-understanding. Help them know themselves, their background and their values. Parents should not be expected to have vast amounts of college expertise, but they would be wise to consult an objective outsider—a counselor—for help, advice, and experienced judgment. Parents should support, respect, love, and affirm the wonderful young people they are about to help launch on their own exciting journeys.

APPENDICES

APPENDIX A

■■■■■■■■■■■■■■■■■■■■■

COLLEGE PLANNING GOALS—
FRESHMAN AND SOPHOMORE YEARS

Freshman Year

- Enjoy school! And not only as a prelude to college but as a place where you are developing as a student and as a person.
- Establish strong study habits and time management techniques.
- Develop a reading plan that includes newspapers, magazines and books.
- Learn where to find reliable information about colleges. (Not all books and websites are equally credible!)
- Work to enhance your reading and writing abilities and vocabulary proficiency.
- Keep your grades up.
- Plan your sophomore year schedule with care. Take classes appropriate for you. Push yourself but know your limits. Colleges look carefully at your classes (and not just your grades). A strong college preparatory program balanced with courses in English, mathematics, social studies, science and languages is important.
- Pursue extracurricular activities and perhaps investigate new activities in which you would like to participate.
- Think about your interests and how those interests might translate into career options. But keep your career options open. Investigate lots of possibilities.
- Pay attention to what friends and others are saying about their college experiences. Think about your own goals for college.
- Meet with your college counselor. Find out about college planning resources available in your school.
- Consider an interesting summer job, travel, or other learning experience.

Sophomore Year

- Meet with your college counselor. Ask what you should do this year to prepare for college.
- Maintain strong study habits and time management techniques.
- Continue to pay attention to college information—websites, books, magazines, etc. Learn where to find reliable information about college.
- Work to enhance your reading and writing abilities and vocabulary proficiency. Assess your writing strengths and weaknesses and work on weaknesses.
- Keep your grades up. Keep copies of your best writing.
- Plan your junior year schedule carefully. Take classes appropriate for you: push yourself but know your limits. Colleges will look carefully at your classes (and not just your grades). A strong, college preparatory program balanced with courses in English, mathematics, social studies, science and languages is important.
- Target major activities. Aim for leadership positions, if appropriate. Keep a record of performances/events/awards.
- Think about those qualities which would make a college right for you. What size is best? Do you have location preferences?
- Pay attention to what friends and others are saying about their college experiences.
- Sit in on a few meetings with college representatives who visit your school.
- Consider teachers who you would like to have write college recommendations for you.
- Some students take preliminary exams this year; the PSAT (to prepare for the SAT) or PLAN (to prepare for the ACT). Ask your counselor.
- Think about your interests and how those interests might translate into career options. But keep your options open. Investigate lots of possibilities.
- Some students take one (or more) SAT Subject Tests in the spring of this year if they are completing a college preparatory subject. Again, consult with your counselor about this.
- Consider an interesting summer job, travel, or other learning experience.

APPENDIX B

■■■■■■■■■■■■■■■■■■■■■

COLLEGE PLANNING GOALS–
JUNIOR YEAR

Preparing For College
- Relax. Approach the college search systematically.
- Keep your grades up.
- Begin/continue a limited number of extracurricular involvements in which you might want to assume leadership roles.
- Plan senior year schedule carefully. Most colleges will look carefully at the breadth and depth of your senior year schedule. Push yourself, but know your limits.
- Work on study skills and time management.
- Complete Activities/Experiences Record (Worksheet 3).
- Think about several career options. Actively investigate a few.
- Talk to your parents about your potential college choices.
- Consider an interesting summer job or travel experience.
- Take every opportunity to improve your writing skills.

Finding Colleges and Preparing to Apply
- Meet with your high school counselor. Find out how college planning operates at your school and identify the resources available to you.
- Label a folder (either a paper one or one on your desktop) "COLLEGE PLANNING.." In it, put important documents related to your college search.
- Identify qualities important in college selection. Complete Worksheets in Chapter 3.
- Attend college representative meetings at school/college night programs/college fairs.
- E-mail colleges for viewbooks and applications.
- Research college choices. Read both objective and subjective types of guidebooks. See Chapter 4.

• Develop a preliminary list of colleges that interest you. Complete
  Worksheet 7.

• Identify and informally talk to teachers about writing a recommendation for you. Think about three teachers: you may ultimately need
  only 1 or 2. Your high school counselor will also likely be asked to
  write a recommendation.

Names of possible recommenders:

_____

_____

_____

• Begin to explore financial aid opportunities. Note resources listed in
  the References section of this book.

• Start work on essay/personal statement preparation. See Chapter 6.

• Consider visits to college campuses—after you speak to your counselor and begin to research potential college choices. See Chapter 5.

Testing Needs

Consider test preparation such as review of sample tests or tutoring.

• PLAN   Test Date_____   Registration Deadline? _____
• PSAT   Test Date _____   Registration Deadline? _____
• SAT   Test Date _____   Registration Deadline? _____
          Test Date _____   Registration Deadline? _____
• ACT   Test Date _____   Registration Deadline? _____
          Test Date _____   Registration Deadline? _____

• SAT Subject Tests. Under test name, list the specific tests you will
  take. For example, Mathematics Level 2 and Chemistry.

Test Name   Test Date   Registration Deadline

_____   _____   _____

_____   _____   _____

Summer Plans

College Planning Goals. Check those you will accomplish.

_____ Investigate my college options

_____ Prepare my list of colleges to which I will apply

_____ Prepare for SATs or ACTs

_____ Refine my list of colleges

_____ Talk with current college students

_____ Write for college applications

_____ Work on my essays

_____ Visits to colleges? Where?

_____ Organize my list of activities

_____ Other. What?

_____ Other. What?

List your summer activities:

_____

_____

_____

_____

_____

_____

_____

_____

_____

_____

_____

Appendix C

College Planning Goals—
Senior Year

Preparing for College

- Keep your "cool" during this year. Systematically move from one phase of the college search to another.
- Keep your grades up. This year *is* important. Remember, many colleges will see your first semester grades and will be impressed if you've taken competitive courses.
- Begin/continue extracurricular involvements.
- Work on study skills and time management.
- Think about several career options. Actively investigate a few.
- Complete Activities/Experiences Record (Worksheet 3).
- Keep your parents informed as to your thinking about your college choices. Seek their counsel.

Finding Colleges and Applying

- Meet regularly with your high school college counselor.
- Identify qualities important in college selection. Complete Worksheets in Chapter 3.
- Attend school/college night programs/college fairs.
- Be sure colleges that you are interested in know that you are interested (e.g., fill out "request for information" forms on college websites).
- Research college choices. Narrow the field. Complete Worksheet 9.
- Use a manila file folder for each college to which you are applying. In it, put copies of the college application and other relevant information.
- Talk to teachers about college recommendations/distribute them. Names of recommenders:

_____

_____

_____

- Work systematically on your applications and essays. Find out precisely what applications, test scores, supplements, etc. are required for all of your college choices.
- Discuss applying "Early Decision" or "Early Action" with your counselor.
- Develop a timetable for application due dates. Complete Worksheet 10.
- Complete and mail applications to colleges. Most students should try to have all applications complete and ready to be mailed in by the end of November. My target date to mail all applications is:

_____

- Practice for college interviews.
- Investigate all relevant scholarship possibilities. Standardized forms are available after Jan. 1. Check with each college for aid information and procedures.
- Consider the best time for college visitations. Where and When?

_____

_____

_____

- Meet housing deadlines.
- Send housing deposit and confirmation to attend.
- SAT   Test Date _____   Registration Deadline? _____
          Test Date _____   Registration Deadline? _____
- ACT   Test Date _____   Registration Deadline? _____
          Test Date _____   Registration Deadline? _____

- SAT Subject Tests. Under test name, list the specific tests you will take. For example, Mathematics Level 2 and Chemistry.

Test Name	Test Date	Registration Deadline
_____	_____	_____
_____	_____	_____

Appendix D

Possible Major Fields of Study*

Accounting
Agricultural Studies
Anthropology
Archaeology
Architecture/Environmental Design
Arts (fine, visual, performing, photography, art history, design, studio etc.)
Astronomy/Planetary Science
Aviation
Biological Sciences
Business Administration and Management
Chemistry
Communications (graphics, advertising, illustration, media, etc.)
Computer Science/Information Sciences
Construction Trades
Criminology
Dance
Economics
Education/Teaching
Engineering (civil, electrical, chemical mechanical, etc.)
English/Creative Writing
Environmental Studies
Ethnic/Cultural Studies (African American, African, Hispanic/Latina/o German, American Indian, East Asian, etc.)
Fashion Design/Merchandising
Film/Television Studies/Media Studies
Geography
Geology/Earth Sciences
Government
Health Sciences/Allied Health (occupational therapy, physical therapy, dental assistant, nursing, etc.)
History
International Studies/Relations
Jewish Studies

Journalism
Languages (Asian, French, Slavic, etc.)
Literature
Marketing
Marine Biology
Mass Communications (media, broadcasting, cable, etc.)
Mathematics
Mechanics and Repairs (of tools, machines, equipment, etc.)
Military Sciences
Music
Philosophy
Physical Education
Physical Sciences
Physics
Political Science
Pre-Professional Studies (pre-engineering, pre-law, pre-med, pre-vet, pre-dental, etc.)
Protection Services (police, fire, etc.)
Psychology
Public Policy
Religious Studies/Theology
Sociology
Speech Communication (interpersonal, group, rhetoric, etc.)
Theatre/Drama
Tourism Industry (hotel administration, restaurant management, etc.)
Transportation (rail, air, water, truck, etc.)
Women's Studies

*Note: There is a distinction between "field of study" and "career." Students choose a field of study on the basis of their interests when they are in high school. A career can be chosen later, after a student has taken a variety of classes in college and learns more about the various vocational options.

APPENDIX E

■ ■

POTENTIAL COLLEGE ACTIVITIES LIST

Check those involvements that have some interest to you

o ACADEMIC CLUBS/ORGANIZATION such as English Society, Business Student Association, Pre-Med Society, Political Science Association, American Society of Civil Engineers, Computer Club

o ADMISSION OFFICE ASSISTANCE such as giving tours, contacting prospective students, developing admission policies

o ATHLETICS/SPORTS/RECREATION such as varsity, club and intramural sports, bicycling, outdoor adventurers, sailing, ultimate Frisbee, climbing club, floor hockey, bowling, video/computer game club, ping-pong

o DEBATE/FORENSICS/PUBLIC SPEAKING

o ENVIRONMENTAL GROUP such as Greenpeace, Rain Forest Action group, Global Change Action group

o FRATERNITY/SORORITY (Greek organizations)

o GOVERNMENT such as residence hall judiciary board, various leadership councils and advisory committees

o INTERNATIONAL STUDENT ORGANIZATIONS/MULTICULTURAL GROUP such as Arab, Italian American, Vietnamese, Latino Student Organization

o JOB (full or part time)

o JOURNALISM/COMMUNICATION such as newspaper, yearbook, literary magazines, other campus publications

o MUSICAL ACTIVITY such as choir, jazz ensemble, marching band, rock band, chamber orchestra

o RADIO/TELEVISION STATION

o RELIGIOUS GROUP

o SOCIAL ACTION/POLITICAL/COMMUNITY SERVICE GROUP such as College Democrats or Republicans, Alliance for Progressive South Asians, Students of Color Coalition, United Students Against Sweatshops, drug or alcohol awareness, Amnesty International, Gay-Straight Alliance, gay and lesbian clubs, Habitat for Humanity, National Organization for Women

o STUDENT CENTER ACTIVITY such as planning for speakers, exhibits, concerts

o THEATER AND ARTS such as drama, dance, visual arts, boogie club, mime group, comedy club

APPENDIX F

■■■■■■■■■■■■■■■■■■■■■

REFERENCES FOR COLLEGE PLANNING

The Application Process

Fiske, Edward B. & Hammond, Bruce G., *Fiske College Deadline Planner: A Week-By-Week Guide to Every Key Deadline*, Sourcebooks, Inc, published annually.

Mathews, Jay, *Harvard Schmarvard: Getting Beyond the Ivy League to the College That is Best for You*, Three River Press, 2003.

Princeton Review, *Guide to College Visits: Planning Trips to Popular Campuses in the Northeast, Southeast, West, and Midwest*, Random House, 2007.

Springer, Sally P. & Franck, Marion R., *Admission Matters: What Students and Parents Need to Know About Getting into College*, John Wiley & Sons, Inc., 2005.

Steinberg, Jacque, *The Gatekeepers: Inside the Admissions Process of a Premier College,* Penguin, 2003.

Tanabe, Gen & Tanabe, Kelly, *Get Into Any College: Secrets of Harvard Students,* Supercollege, LLC, 2006

Van Buskirk, Peter, *Winning the College Admission Game: Strategies for Parents & Students.* Peterson's, 2007.

Guidebooks: Comprehensive

Barron's Profiles of American Colleges, Barron's Educational Series, Inc, published annually.

College Admissions Data Sourcebooks, Wintergreen Orchard House, published annually.

College Handbook, College Board, published annually.

Peterson's Four-Year Colleges, published annually.

Peterson's Two-Year Colleges, published annually.

Guidebooks: Subjective Reviews

Fiske, Edward B., *Fiske Guide to Colleges.* Sourcebooks, Inc., published annually.

Goldman, Jordan & Buyers, Colleen, *Students' Guide to Colleges: The Definitive Guide to America's Top 100 Schools Written by the Real Experts—The Students Who Attended Them*, Penguin, 2005.

Pope, Loren, *Colleges That Change Lives: 40 Schools That Will Change the Way You Think About Colleges,* Penguin, 2006.

Pope, Loren, *Looking Beyond the Ivy League: Finding the College That's Right for You*, Penguin, 2007.

Princeton Review *Best 368 Colleges*, Random House Inc., published annually.

Yale Daily News Staff, *The Insider's Guide to the Colleges*, Macmillan, published annually.

Zmirak, John, *Choosing the Right College: 2008-2009: The Whole Truth About America's 100 Top Schools*, Intercollegiate Studies Institute, published most years.

College Costs & Financial Aid

Cassidy, Daniel J. (Editor), *The Scholarship Book*. New York: Prentice Hall Press, published annually.

College Cost & Financial Aid Handbook, New York: College Board Publications.

Leider, Anna, *The A's and B's of Academic Scholarships*. Alexandria, VA: Octameron Associates, published bi-annually.

Leider, Robert & Anna Leider, *Don't Miss Out: The Ambitious Student's Guide to Financial Aid*, Octameron Associates, published annually.

Guidebooks: Specialized

Antonoff, Steven, *The College Finder,* Wintergreen Orchard House, 2008.

Arthur, Priscilla & Bradshaw, Matt, *The College Atlas and Planner*, Wintergreen Orchard House, 2005.

Asher, Donald, *Cool Colleges: For the Hyper-Intelligent, Self-Directed, Late Blooming and Just Plain Different*. Ten Speed Press, 2007.

Bender, Sheila, *Perfect Phrases for College Application Essays*, McGraw-Hill, 2008.

Buez, John; Howd, Jennifer; Pepper, Rachel & The Princeton Review Staff, *The Gay and Lesbian Guide to College Life: A Comprehensive Resource for Lesbian, Gay, Bisexual and Transgender Students and Their Allies*, Random House, 2007.

Christian Colleges & Universities: The Official Guide to Campuses of the Council for Christian Colleges & Universities, Peterson's, published most years.

Colleges with a Conscience: 81 Great Schools with Outstanding Community Involvement, Princeton Review/Random House, 2005.

Eliscu, Jenny, *Schools That Rock: The Rolling Stone College Guide*, Wenner Media, 2005.

Fiske, Edward B., *Fiske Real College Essays That Work*, Sourcebooks, Inc., 2006.

MacLeans Guide To Canadian Universities, published annually.

McGinty, Sarah M., *The College Application Essay*, College Board, 2007.

Orr, Tamra B., *America's Best Colleges for B Students: A College Guide for Students Without Straight A's*, Supercollege, LLC, 2005.

Professor Pathfinder's U.S. College and University Reference Map., Hedberg Maps, Inc. 2006.

Valverde, Leonard A., *The Latino Student's Guide to College Success*, Greenwood Publishing Group, 2001.

Weinstein, Miriam, *Making a Difference College & Graduate Guide*, Sage Works Press, 2004.

Windmeyer, Shane L., *The Advocate College Guide for LGBT Students*, Alyson Books, 2006.

Majors, Academic Programs & Careers

Asher, Donald, *How to Get Any Job With Any Major: Career Launch & Re-Launch for Everyone Under 30 or (How to Avoid Living in Your Parent's Basement)*, Ten Speed Press, 2004.

Book of Majors, College Board, published annually.

Fenza, D.W., *The AWP Official Guide to Writing Programs*. Dustbooks, published annually.

Fogg, Neeta P., Harrington, Paul E. & Harrington, Thomas F., *College Majors Handbook with Real Career Paths and Payoffs: The Actual Jobs, Earnings and Trends for Graduates of 60 College Majors*, JIST Works, 2004.

Forster, Stephanie, *Dance Magazine College Guide*, Dance Magazine, Inc., published annually.

Gardner, Garth, *Gardner's Guide to Colleges for Multimedia & Animation*, Garth Gardner Co.

Index of Majors & Sports, Wintergreen-Orchard House, published annually.

Journalist's Road to Success: A Career Guide, Dow Jones Newspaper Fund, 2002.

Kahn, Russell & Weiss, Jodi, *145 Things to Be When You Grow Up*, Princeton Review, 2004.

Levine, Mel, *Ready or Not, Here Life Comes*, Simon & Schuster, 2005.

Loveland, Elaina, *Creative Colleges: A Guide for Student Actors, Artists, Dancers, Musicians and Writers*, Supercollege, LLC, 2005.

Peterson's Professional Degree Programs in the Visual & Performing Arts, published every few years.

Phifer, Paul, *College Majors and Careers: A Resource Guide for Effective Life Planning*, Ferguson Publishing, 2003.

Rugg, Fredrick E., *Rugg's Recommendations on the Colleges*, published annually.

Taylor, Jeffrey & Hardy, Douglass, *Monster Careers: How to Land the Job of Your Life*, Penguin, 2004.

Zichy, Shoya & Bidou, Ann, *Career Match: Connecting Who You Are with What You'll Love to Do*, AMACOM, 2007.

Athletics

Hastings, Penny & Caven, Todd D., *How to Win a Sports Scholarship*. Redwood Creek Publishing, 2007.

National Directory of College Athletics, Collegiate Directories, published annually.

Nitardy, Nancy, *Get Paid to Play: Every Student Athlete's Guide to Over $1 Million in College Scholarships*. Kaplan Publishing, 2007.

Peterson's Sports Scholarships and College Athletic Programs, published most years.

Learning Disabilities/Differences

Colleges for Students with Learning Disabilities or ADD, Peterson's, published most years.

Kravets, Marybeth & Wax, Imy F., *The K & W Guide to Colleges for Students with Learning Disabilities or Attention Deficit Disorder*, Princeton Review, published every few years.

Lipkin, Midge, *College Sourcebook For Students with Learning and Developmental Differences*, Wintergreen Orchard House, published every few years.

Parent Guides

Coburn, Karen L. & Treeger, Madge L., *Letting Go: A Parent's Guide to Understanding the College Years*, HarperCollins, 2003.

Jones, Marilee, Ginsburg, Kenneth R. & Jablow, Martha M., *Less Stress, More Success: A New Approach to Guiding Your Teen Through College Admissions and Beyond*, American Academy of Pediatrics, 2006.

Kastner, Laura S. & Wyatt, Jennifer F., *The Launching Years: Strategies for Parenting from Senior Year to College Life*, Three Rivers Press, 2002.

Koplewicz, Harold S., *More Than Moody: Recognizing and Treating Adolescent Depression*, Putnam Adult, 2003.

Raskin, Robin, *Parents' Guide to College Life: 181 Straight Answers on Everything you Can Expect Over the Next Four Years*, Princeton Review, 2006.

Rubenstone, Sally & Dalby, Sidonia, *Panicked Parents' Guide to College Admissions*, Petersons, 2002.

Schoensein, Ralph, *Toilet Trained for Yale: Adventures in 21st-Century Parenting.*, Da Capo Press, 2002.

Other Resources

440 Great Colleges for Top Students, Peterson's, published most every year.

Boyer, Paul, *College Rankings Exposed: The Art of Getting a Quality Education in the 21st Century*, Petersons, 2003.

Burnette, Dawn, *High School 101: Freshman Survival Guide.* United Writers Press, Inc., 2005.

Career Opportunities News, published six times per year by Ferguson Publishing Company, fergpubco.com.

Carter, Carol, *Making the Most of High School: Success Secrets for Freshman,* Lifebound, 2004.

Covey, Sean, *The 7 Habits of Highly Effective Teenagers,* Fireside, 1998.

Digby, John, *Peterson's Smart Choices: Honors Programs and Colleges*, Petersons, 2005.

Google's University Search tool, google.com/options/universities

Hewitt, Les, Hewitt, Andrew, d'Abadie, Luc & Trump, Donald, *The Power of Focus for College Students: How to Make College the Best Investment of Your Life*, HCI, 2005.

Light, Richard, *Making the Most of College: Students Speak Their Minds*, Harvard University Press, 2001.

Peterson's Summer Opportunities for Kids & Teenagers, Petersons.

Schoem, David, *College Knowledge: 101 Tips for the College-Bound Student*, University of Michigan Press, 2005.

Spires, Jeanette, *What Do You Know: Wisdom for the Road Ahead*, Riverwood Books, 2004.

Thacker, Lloyd, *College Unranked: Ending the College Admissions Frenzy*, Harvard University Press, 2005.

College Planning Guides from Octameron

Don't Miss Out: The Ambitious Student's Guide to Financial Aid **$13.00**
Hailed as the top consumer guide to student aid, *Don't Miss Out* covers scholarships, loans, and personal finance strategies. It will save readers hundreds, if not thousands of dollars in college costs.

The A's and B's of Academic Scholarships **$13.00**
Money for being bright! This book describes 100,000 awards offered by nearly 1200 colleges. Best of all, most of these (which must be used at the sponsoring school) are not based on financial need.

Loans and Grants from Uncle Sam **$8.00**
Increase your eligibility for federal student aid. This guide describes it all—the aid application process as well as loans and grants for students, parents and health professionals.

Financial Aid FinAncer: Expert Answers to College Financing Questions **$8.00**
Learn how special family circumstances impact on student aid.

The Winning Edge: The Student-Athlete's Guide to College Sports **$9.00**
It's all here. Scholarship opportunities. NCAA rules and regulations. Advice from coaches. Sample athletic resumes. Strategies, timetables, and worksheets—all to help you take your sport to college!

Financial Aid Officers: What They Do—To You and For You **$5.00**
Should you accept your award package as offered? Can you request it be changed, or increased? Knowledgeable dealings with FAOs can result in more money. This book shows you how.

Behind the Scenes: An Inside Look at the College Admission Process **$8.00**
Ed Wall, former Dean of Admission at Amherst College, offers sage advice and detailed profiles of successful applicants. An invaluable view from inside on how the selection process really works.

Do It Write: How to Prepare a Great College Application **$7.00**
Personalize your essays so they stand out from the crowd. Author Gary Ripple is the former Admission Director at Lafayette College and the College of William and Mary

College Match: A Blueprint for Choosing the Best School for You **$12.00**
Author Steve Antonoff combines dozens of easy-to-use worksheets with lots of practical advice to make sure you find schools that meet your needs and your preferences.

Campus Pursuit: Making the Most of the Visit and Interview **$6.00**
Nervous about your interview? In his companion book to *Do-It Write*, Gary Ripple gives advice that will help you shine, as well as show you how to maximize the benefits of a campus visit.

College.edu: On-Line Resources for the Cyber-Savvy Student **$12.00**
Lost in Cyberspace? *College.edu* takes you to hundreds of useful sites on admission and financial aid, giving you Internet tips and warnings along the way.

Campus Daze: Easing the Transition from High School to College **$8.00**
Learn what to expect during your first year of college and how to succeed starting on Day One. Author George Gibbs is the former Dean of Admission and Freshmen at Muhlenberg College.

College Majors That Work **$10.00**
Get in. Get out. Get a job. Worksheets help match a student's goals and expectations with the right college major and explores how that choice plays out in the real world—influencing both career and lifestyle options. Written by Michael P. Viollt, President of Robert Morris College (IL),

Calculating Expected Family Contribution (EFC) Software **$45.00**
Estimate how much you will be expected to pay for college. This Windows-compatible CD-Rom software holds data on hundreds of families and let's you analyze different income and asset scenarios.

Ordering Information

Send Orders to: Octameron Associates, PO Box 2748, Alexandria, VA 22301, or contact us at: 703-836-5480 (voice), 703-836-5650 (fax), octameron@aol.com (e-mail).

Order Online: www.octameron.com.

Postage and Handling: Please include $3.00 for one publication, $5.00 for two publications $6.00 for three publications and $7.00 for four or more publications.

Method of Payment: Payment must accompany order. We accept checks, money orders, American Express, Visa and MasterCard.

If ordering by credit card, please include the card number and its expiration date.